The
TROPICAL
MARINE FISH
Survival Manual

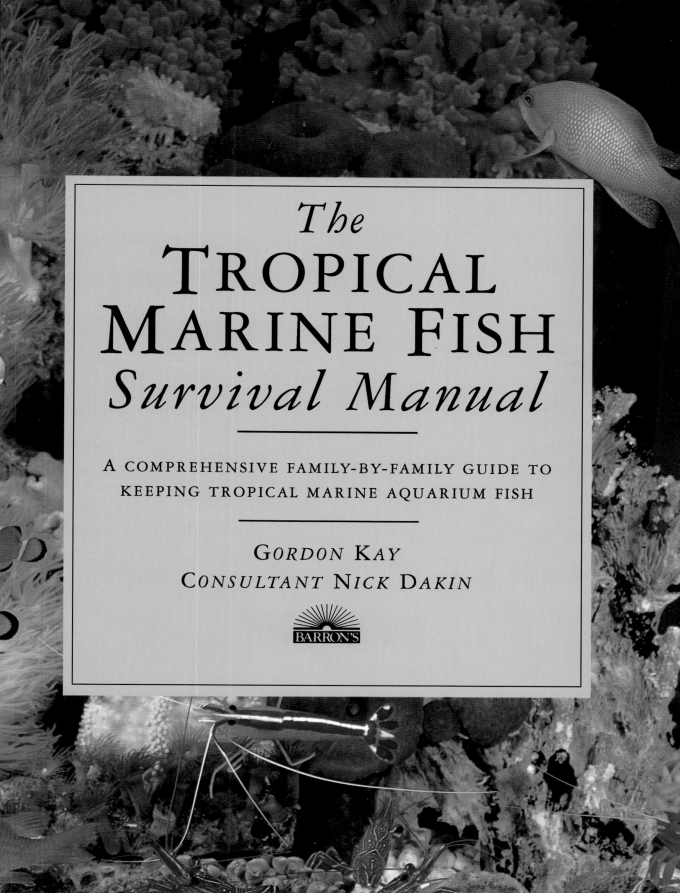

The
TROPICAL
MARINE FISH
Survival Manual

A COMPREHENSIVE FAMILY-BY-FAMILY GUIDE TO
KEEPING TROPICAL MARINE AQUARIUM FISH

GORDON KAY
CONSULTANT NICK DAKIN

BARRON'S

A Quarto Book
Copyright © 1995 Quarto Inc., London

First U.S. edition published in 1995 by
Barron's Educational Series, Inc.

All enquiries should be addressed to:
Barron's Educational Series, Inc.
250 Wireless Boulevard, Hauppauge, NY 11788

International Standard Book No. 0-8120-9372-0

Reprinted 1997, 1998, 1999, 2000, 2001, 2002 (twice)

9 8

Library of Congress Catalog No. 95-21172

Designed and produced by
Quarto Inc.
The Old Brewery, 6 Blundell Street
London N7 9BH

SENIOR EDITOR Maria Morgan
EDITOR Helen Douglas-Cooper
ART EDITOR Liz Brown
DESIGNERS Geoff Manders, Sheila Volpe,
Allan Mole
ILLUSTRATORS Chris Orr, Dave Kemp
PICTURE RESEARCH MANAGER Giulia Hetherington
ART DIRECTOR Moira Clinch
EDITORIAL DIRECTOR Mark Dartford

Typeset by Central Southern Typesetters, Eastbourne
Manufactured in Hong Kong by Regent
Publishing Services Ltd.
Printed in China by Leefung-Asco Printers Ltd.

The publishers would like to point out that several
species included in this book produce venom and
are therefore potentially dangerous to humans.
Information and recommendations are given without
any guarantees on the part of the author, consultant,
and publisher, and they cannot be held responsible
for any unforeseen circumstances.

SECTION ONE:
AN INTRODUCTION TO THE
MARINE FISH AQUARIUM....8

THE ENVIRONMENT
PHYSIOLOGY
CORALFISHES
SPECIFIC GRAVITY
SELECTING AN AQUARIUM
HEATING THE AQUARIUM
LIGHTING THE AQUARIUM
FLUORESCENT TUBES
MERCURY VAPOR
METAL HALIDE
FILTRATION
UNDERGRAVEL FILTERS
REVERSE-FLOW UNDERGRAVEL FILTERS
TRICKLE FILTRATION
ACTIVATED CARBON
PROTEIN SKIMMING
ULTRAVIOLET STERILIZERS
MATURING THE BIOLOGICAL FILTER
WATER QUALITY AND TESTING
MEASURING SALINITY
pH IN THE AQUARIUM

CONTENTS

INTRODUCTION

*I*f the evolution of the Earth was charted on a clock face, the human race's time on the planet to date would span the section from 10 to 12. However, if human knowledge of the world were charted in the same way, our understanding of the sea would span an even shorter time. For instance, we have only recently begun to understand the mechanism for the fantastic color and pattern changes in Cephalopods – octopuses, squid and cuttlefishes. Similarly, we have only recently understood how to keep coral animals successfully in captivity. Having said that, we have learned these things very quickly, so quickly, in fact, that the marine aquarium hobby is experimenting with and introducing new techniques to fishkeeping generally.

As a result, it is now no more difficult to keep marine species than it is to keep guppies. This book endeavors to provide readers with the necessary knowledge to maintain a successful marine aquarium, in a form that is easy to understand, so that they can experience the delights that some of us have enjoyed for years. Although there has been a phenomenal increase in the popularity of invertebrates – animals without backbones – during the past decade, the beginner should keep only fishes for the year or so. Invertebrate aquariums can be an exacting science, requiring far more skill and experience than the beginner can muster. For this reason, apart from a few passing mentions, this book includes no discussion of invertebrates.

The marine aquarium This beautiful and serene underwater world is no longer a mystery. Certainly a lot of time, thought, care and hard work is needed, but the results are definitely worth the effort.

HOW TO USE THIS BOOK

The book is divided into five sections, together giving comprehensive guidance to the beginner marine-fish aquarist. The first part is a general introduction to the hobby, including basic information that beginners should know – the physiology of fish, the components of a tank and their functions, filters, heating and lighting and the importance of water quality.

Sections two and three concentrate on setting up and maintaining an aquarium, including what to look for when buying fish and general guidance on feeding.

Section four is a directory of 33 fish families with advice on the care of species most commonly seen in the hobby. Each fish is key-coded with simple symbols. Check the symbols against the key given at the start of each family (see right).

Section five deals with potential problems and their solutions, including advice on aquarium maintenance and how to recognize and treat diseases.

Key symbols

The maximum length attained by the fish in its natural habitat

Maximum length likely in an aquarium

Should only be fed vegetable-based foods

Eats all types of aquarium foods

A meat-eater likely to attack other fishes

Should not be kept with others of the same species, possibly territorial

Best kept in groups of its own kind

No danger to smaller fishes, even if a large species

Peaceful, delicate species harmless to other tank-dwellers

The higher the number, the easier the species is to keep by a beginner

KEY

LENGTH IN WILD(INS)

LENGTH IN CAPTIVITY (INS)

HERBIVORE

OMNIVORE

PREDATOR

SINGLE SPECIMEN

COMMUNITY

SAFE WITH SMALL FISHES

SAFE WITH INVERTEBRATES

EASE OF KEEPING (SCALE OF 1 -10)

7

Key to symbols used for each species

Scientific and common name of family, with general introduction

Distribution of all family members indicated by darker map areas

General information on species, including natural and captive behavior

Question and answer panel addressing common problems

Scientific and common name of species, with key symbols

AN INTRODUCTION TO THE MARINE FISH AQUARIUM

The two main differences between marine and freshwater creatures are the type of water in which they live and the physiology of the animals themselves. There are also fundamental differences in relation to both. Freshwater fishes live in rivers, lakes and other inland waterways, and because factors such as too little or too much rainfall and evaporation affect their environment, they have to be able to adapt to changing conditions, sometimes very quickly. They have, therefore, evolved in a way that allows them to make such adaptations. In contrast, the coral reef is the most stable environment on Earth and the animals that live on it have never needed to evolve such mechanisms. There are some species of coralfish to which a change of as little as 0.001 in specific gravity (salinity) or 0.1 in pH (acidity or alkalinity) could be fatal. Marine aquariology has earned a reputation for being difficult, but, with a little basic knowledge, the subject becomes more straightforward.

THE ENVIRONMENT

The amount of dissolved material in water varies from one area to another in both marine and freshwater habitats and, though sodium chloride – common salt – is the main constituent in seawater, it is not the only one. It would be far more precise to say that marine

Coral reef
The coral reef is the most stable environment on Earth.

habitats are those in which the concentration of dissolved salts is greater in the water than that found within the cells of organisms living in it. Concentrations of these dissolved salts in fresh water are always lower than within the cells of the animals living in that water.

All living things must maintain their body cells' chemical composition within very precise limits, and because cell membranes are selectively permeable, water will cross from areas of low salinity to those of high salinity in an attempt to even things up. This process is known as osmosis and creates a significant survival challenge to both freshwater and seawater animals. Freshwater fishes are in constant danger of being "flooded" by their environment, because the higher concentrations of salts in their body cells could draw in water from their surroundings. Seawater fishes, on the other hand, risk dehydration because the higher concentration of salts in the waters in which they live could draw water out of their body cells. Because the raw materials of chemical synthesis and the resulting waste products must be able to move across cell membranes, the development of impermeable barriers to prevent flooding or dehydration is not the answer. Any mechanism developed to deal with the problem in hand must be active, rather than passive.

PHYSIOLOGY

Freshwater fishes address the issue by "waterproofing" as many of their body surfaces – both internal and external – as possible and swallowing very little water. Even then, large quantities of water are absorbed across the surface of the gills, although highly efficient kidneys make up for this by producing copious amounts of very dilute urine.

Even here there is a risk of depleting the body's reserves of ions (calcium, potassium and so on), which are needed for normal cellular function. However, these are reabsorbed by the wall of the urinary bladder. By cutting down the loss of these substances, any deficiency is made up by the fish's food.

Marine fishes deal with the threat of dehydration in several ways. The Elasmobranchs (sharks and rays) regulate osmotic activity by allowing the concentration of dissolved salts in their body fluids to exceed that of their environment through the retention of urea and other metabolic wastes, which puts them in a similar position to freshwater fishes. However, they lack the salt-recycling mechanism of freshwater fishes and their urine is somewhat concentrated as a result.

Bony fishes – which constitute the majority of marine species – drink constantly to make up for the water that they lose to their environment. Coralfishes take in as much as 35 percent of their own body weight every day. Calcium, magnesium and other heavy ions remain in the gut because they have a double electrical charge, but sodium, chloride and potassium pass into the body fluids and are excreted by "chloride cells" in the gills. As seawater fishes have the problem of retaining rather than eliminating water, they have fairly inefficient kidneys that produce small amounts of highly concentrated urine.

The implications of this aspect of marine-fish physiology in regard to their aquarium well-being are immense. It should be clear by now why a freshwater fish can't be kept in a seawater aquarium. It should also be clear that salt excretion requires a vast amount of energy on the part of marine fish to function properly. This fact alone explains why coralfish have enormous appetites, and why they do better when fed small amounts of food regularly. Furthermore, their systems are finely tuned to external conditions and are easily upset by abrupt changes in salinity. Finally, it should also be obvious that all water taken in by aquarium fish needs to be of the highest possible quality.

Osmosis

Freshwater fish absorb water through the skin. It is excreted in large amounts to prevent a build-up in the body. In contrast, marine fish lose water through their skin and drink heavily to compensate.

Freshwater fish

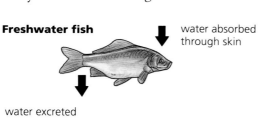

water absorbed through skin

water excreted

Marine fish

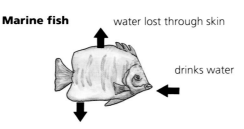

water lost through skin

drinks water

water lost through skin

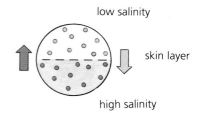

low salinity

skin layer

high salinity

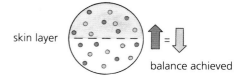

skin layer

balance achieved

Osmosis is the process whereby organic cells have the capacity to expel or absorb water in order to achieve a balance of salinity

CORALFISHES IN THE AQUARIUM

In recent years it has generally been thought advantageous to maintain aquarium salinities at a level a little below those found on the coral reefs. A lower salt concentration lessens the burden on aquarium fishes considerably, because it reduces the stress that salt excretion places upon them. Owing to the amount of dissolved solids in seawater, its capacity to retain oxygen is considerably less than that of fresh water. On the reef, water is constantly agitated and always absorbing oxygen from the air. Therefore, fishes haven't evolved a mechanism for dealing with reduced oxygen levels. Fortunately, a reduction in the salinity of water in an aquarium allows the water to retain more oxygen, thus reducing the problem, and good aeration techniques will help to eradicate it completely. Further trouble can crop up in summer, when high temperatures reduce seawater's oxygen-dissolving capacity

even further while increasing the fishes' respiratory demands. Low salinity will help to reduce stress in the fish to a minimum. One other thought to bear in mind regarding salinity is that small bodies of seawater have a habit of becoming increasingly salty due to evaporation. A low initial salinity level reduces the risk of fishes becoming exposed to increasingly stressful levels of salinity over a period of time.

WHAT IS SPECIFIC GRAVITY?

Put simply, specific gravity (S.G.) is a measure of the density of seawater. The greater the specific gravity, the higher the level of salt dissolved in the water. Distilled water – which has no dissolved salts – has a specific gravity of 1.000. Seawater with a specific gravity of 1.024 is, therefore, 1.024 times as dense as distilled water. Specific gravity is easier to measure if you use a proprietary hydrometer (see pages 26–27), which can be bought from any aquarium shop.

Coralfish
This is the look we are ultimately aiming for – a healthy tropical marine aquarium with compatible fish.

SELECTING AN AQUARIUM

The first requirement is a proper glass tank, along with an assortment of hardware. The necessary equipment is discussed on the following pages, but the tank (aquarium) should be talked about first. Many books still refer to metal-framed and acrylic tanks. It is highly unlikely, however, that you would see a metal-framed aquarium on sale today. This is just as well, because seawater is extremely corrosive and the effects of heavy metal poisoning on the fishes would be fatal. New, scratch-resistant acrylic tanks are now becoming more widely available in some countries.

It is a mistake to buy a small aquarium "just to get started." Always choose the largest aquarium that you can afford and have space for. In a new aquarium, water quality will be unstable and we have already seen that coralfishes cannot cope easily with fluctuations in conditions. In a large aquarium, conditions will change more slowly, and changes will have less impact on the fish as a result. It is also easier to achieve stability with a large aquarium. In any event, it is wisest to buy an aquarium that is 91 cm x 46 cm high x 46 cm deep (36 in x 18 in x 18 in) at the very minimum.

The natural behavior of coralfishes should also be taken into consideration. Although freshwater fishes sometimes display territorial behavior, there are groups that never do so. For those that do, it is usually a function of reproduction activity or in defense of a shelter. Either way, it should be easily managed. In coralfishes, on the other hand, persistant territorial behavior is a basic characteristic. If a secure food source is being defended, reef fishes can be most intolerant of other individuals of the same species. However, they will also turn on species with similar feeding patterns to their own. It follows, therefore, that fishes for the aquarium must be chosen with their behavior and feeding patterns in mind. The space available also has a distinct bearing on how aggressive they will be, for example, if they cannot form their own "niches."

Another important consideration with regard to aquarium size is its surface area. Oxygen enters the water

Basic aquarium

An all-glass aquarium is the only real choice for the serious hobbyist. Buy the largest one you can afford.

and – probably more important – noxious gases such as carbon dioxide escape into the air at the water surface. Therefore, the larger the surface area, the more efficient the exchange of gases will be. Two aquariums have the same water capacity – for example, one measuring 91 cm long x 46 cm wide x 61 cm deep (36 in x 18 in x 24 in), and the other measuring 91 cm long x 61 cm wide x 46 cm deep (36 in x 24 in x 18 in). However, the first tank has a surface area of 4186 cm^2 (648 in^2), whereas the second has a surface area of 5551 cm^2 (864 in^2). Buy the second aquarium because it has better gas exchange.

In addition to size and surface area, the shape of the aquarium should also be taken into account. In addition to the usual rectangular shape, bow-fronted, hexagonal, octagonal and even trapezoidal tanks can be obtained. However, the latter all have their problems. Not only can they make for distorted viewing, they can be difficult to light, the fish in them may find it

hard to establish territories or even swim properly, and they are also harder to clean. Surface area could also be compromised by an unusual shape.

As well as an aquarium, you will need something to stand it on and this, again, requires some thought. Filled with water, decorations and equipment, the aquarium will be very heavy. For instance, an aquarium containing just 135 liters (30 gal) can weigh over 200 kg (500 lb). That sort of weight carried on a stand with just four legs is not only unstable, but because the total weight is concentrated down the legs, it will ruin a carpet. If it is standing on wooden floorboards, the aquarium could even end up in the basement. Almost all stores sell aquarium cabinets – some with integrated hoods – specially made to carry the tanks that they sell. Whatever you choose to put the aquarium on, make sure that it will carry the weight, will spread it over as large an area as possible and that it is positioned at right angles to any wooden floor joists.

Aquarium with hood and stand
Tanks come in all shapes and sizes. Some can be mounted on display stands or cabinets but, because of the weight, larger ones must have a more solid support. A hood is essential if keeping boisterous species.

Heating the Aquarium

In temperate countries, a tropical seawater aquarium needs to be heated and the most important consideration is temperature stability. In the wild, coralfishes are exposed to minimal temperature variations over a 24-hour period, although seasonal variations between 22° and 30°C (72°–86°F) are common. When the water temperature drops below 20°C (68°F) coralfishes become sluggish, less aggressive and eat far less. At the other end of the scale, at temperatures above 30°C (86°F), they become far more active than usual and their appetites and aggression are stimulated to match. Remember also that the lifespan of fishes is shortened in higher temperatures because their metabolic rate is increased greatly. In captivity, a good compromise is within a temperature range of 24–27°C (75°–81°F).

Heater and thermostat

The neatest and most convenient way to heat the aquarium is with a combined heater and thermostat. A stick-on thermometer is the safest way to measure water temperature.

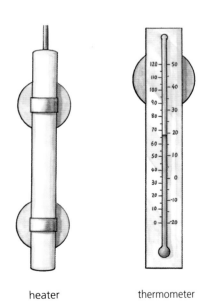

heater   thermometer

The criteria to apply when choosing equipment are that it is accurate and reliable enough to keep the temperature as stable as possible and that it is suitable for use in seawater. All aquarium heaters consist of glass tubes containing a heater element and a sealed bung to keep out water. However, the heat that is produced has to be controlled and this is done either by a separate thermostat, which is wired to the heater and sits elsewhere in or outside the aquarium, or by a thermostat that is incorporated into the same tube – a combined heater/thermostat. For accuracy, convenience and aesthetic value, the combined units are preferable. Digitally controlled heater/thermostat units with a control knob on top for adjusting the setting are now available. This type of unit is more expensive, but more reliable.

The power of a heater is measured in watts – the higher the wattage, the more powerful the heater. Usually, a 100-watt unit will heat a minimum-sized tank, with a 200-watt unit heating a 360 liter (80 gal) tank and a 300-watt unit heating a 680 liter (150 gal) aquarium. It is best to use two heaters, each providing half the total wattage required. The use of a heater at each end of the aquarium ensures an even spread of heat around the tank. If one heater is set at a degree or two lower than the other and if one heater should fail in the "OFF" position, then the other would prevent the fishes being affected by cold. On the other hand, if one of the heaters fails in the "ON" position, it isn't powerful enough to cook the inhabitants.

Even with extremely accurate heaters and thermostats, the temperature needs monitoring with a thermometer. Never

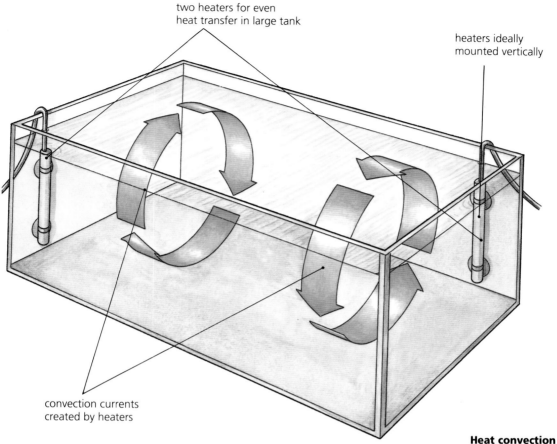

two heaters for even
heat transfer in large tank

heaters ideally
mounted vertically

convection currents
created by heaters

Heat convection

In a large tank, mount
two heaters for even
heat transfer. Here they
are on the back and
side of the tank, but
both can be mounted
along the back out of
the way. The arrows
show the convection
currents generated by
the heaters.

use a mercury thermometer in a
seawater aquarium because, should the
mercury leak into the aquarium water, it
would kill everything in the tank. It is
far safer, and neater, to use a modern,
stick-on thermometer. In fact, it is wise
to use two here also. With a
thermometer at either end of the
aquarium, one near the base and one
near the surface, you can get a complete
picture of the heat flow around the tank.
Any cold spots can be easily eradicated
by adjusting filter outlets or moving air
diffusers.

LIGHTING THE AQUARIUM

Whether you keep only fish species in your first year, or include invertebrates from the start, the aquarium needs light. On a coral reef the animals enjoy hours of intense sunlight, which is further enhanced by the fact that the water is crystal clear and relatively shallow. In the aquarium, therefore, this light level needs to be replicated. This means a minimum of 12 hours of light – 14 hours is preferable – and a period of darkness. Attempts to alter the pattern present so many problems, such as keeping the aquarium dark enough during the day, that it is not worth interfering with the daylight/darkness pattern of the place where you live. Lighting fish-only aquariums is fairly straightforward, since you only have to supply enough light to view the fishes and for them to go about their daily business. In invertebrate aquariums, however, lighting is a far more complicated issue, and if you want to keep these animals, you should consult a book that deals with the topic in depth before going any further.

Mercury vapor lamps

These are pendant-type lamps suspended over the tank. They produce an attractive effect and, like metal halide lamps, encourage algal growth.

Fluorescent tubes

Although the most popular source of aquarium lighting in the hobby, they do give the tank a somewhat dull appearance, detracting from the presentation.

Metal halide lamps

A highly intensive light source but very expensive to run. They are also known as tungsten-halogen or quartz-halogen lamps.

There is, unfortunately, nothing really like natural sunlight for showing the wonderful colors of coralfishes at their best. However, if you live in a climate where the sunlight is unpredictable, you will need some kind of artificial lighting. There are several ways to achieve this and we shall look at one or two of them in a moment. Before we do that, however, there are some basic rules that apply to them all. First, lighting must be supplied in a way that will replicate nature, by providing a pattern of light and dark. It is totally unnatural to provide light for 24 hours every day in order to make up for low light levels. In addition to supplying the correct pattern and intensity of light, you should ensure that the light is of the correct spectrum (or color). In other words, quality is as important as quantity. Whichever type of lighting you choose, it is important that it is of a similar color spectrum to that of the sun. Beneficial green algae are scarce in an aquarium, and with lighting of the wrong type and intensity, undesirable types of algae – brown and red – will start to appear as water quality deteriorates. Red light is filtered out very quickly in nature, so lighting that tends towards this end of the spectrum is useless in the aquarium. Finally, high levels of light would be inappropriate in an aquarium containing only nocturnal species or species that live in caves. Before you make a decision about the type of lighting you buy, therefore, think about the species you will ultimately be keeping.

FLUORESCENT TUBES

This is the most popular method of lighting an aquarium, as fluorescent tubes are inexpensive to run and cool in operation. However, they give an even spread of light that does not create the rippling effect obtained with other types of light. This is the best method of lighting for a fish-only aquarium, nevertheless, because of the advantages already mentioned and the fact that they are easy to install in an aquarium hood. Each tube will need a starter unit to fire it, like any household fluorescent tube.

The choice of fluorescent tubes can be confusing since tubes of a similar color are marketed under varying trade names around the world. Use full-spectrum white lights, designed for the aquarium hobby. They are available in a range of sizes to suit most aquarium lengths. A 61 cm (24 in) long tube will have a rating of 20 watts, a 91 cm (36 in) tube 30 watts, and so on. Usually, two tubes of a similar length to the aquarium itself will suffice. However, to ensure that any algae that may grow will be of the desired green variety, a third tube may be required. A third tube will certainly be required if your aquarium is deeper than 61 cm (24 in).

Tubes are available now that have been developed specifically for use in the marine aquarium. These new triphosphor tubes concentrate their output in the areas of the spectrum essential to marine life, and are aesthetically pleasing to the eye. Their greatest advantage, though, is that they maintain the correct spectral output throughout their lives, whereas more conventional tubes have to be replaced every six months or so.

MERCURY VAPOR
These are spotlights that use mercury vapor to produce light and have a consumption of between 80 and 125 watts, depending on the model. These lamps give a choice of bulb between one with a built-in reflector and one with an external reflector. The main advantage of mercury vapor lighting is that it can illuminate deeper aquariums. It also gives a pleasing ripple effect when used in tanks with high water-surface movement. However, mercury-vapor lighting also has its drawbacks. The life of the bulbs is very short, with output dropping by as much as half over a six-month period, so running costs can be high. They must be positioned at least 30 cm (12 in) above the water surface, because they will shatter if splashed. Finally, the spectral output of mercury vapor leaves much to be desired, lacking output in the blue/green area.

METAL HALIDE
This form of lighting is becoming increasingly popular with keepers of invertebrate aquariums since it gives a light of great intensity. However, it is extremely expensive to buy and to run, with wattages of around 150 being the most common. It has a very high ultraviolet content, which can be harmful to humans, and runs at a very high temperature. Still, many reef-aquarium keepers consider this type of lighting essential for keeping creatures such as corals and anemones.

Whichever type of lighting you choose, both the equipment and its operating efficiency will be damaged by water splashing around in the aquarium. All connections must be protected with waterproof devices to protect the electrical supply and aquarium keeper. Tight-fitting cover glasses should be installed between the water surface and the lamp to protect the equipment and to cut down on evaporation caused by heat from the lights. These cover glasses must be kept spotless. If you buy a combined aquarium and cabinet, cover glasses are usually included.

FILTRATION

The most important skill in keeping coralfishes successfully is the management of the nitrogen cycle in the aquarium. Their failure to understand the sensitivity of marine animals to ammonia – and to a lesser extent, nitrite – meant that all the efforts of the Victorian aquarists were doomed to failure. The inability of coralfishes to cope with even tiny amounts of these substances is due to the fact that they never encounter them in the wild. The combination of the huge amount of water in the ocean, water circulation and the nutrient recycling system on coral reefs keeps concentrations of ammonia and nitrite to levels that are so minute as to be virtually non-existent. Marine organisms have never evolved the ability to deal with these substances because they haven't had to.

Many freshwater habitats, especially in tropical areas, are plagued by variations in volume and rates of water flow. During the dry season, by-products of the nitrogen cycle will frequently accumulate in areas of restricted water movement, such as swamps, oxbows and even the main channel of very sizable rivers. The onset of rain, with its flushing action, soon puts the situation right, but animals that live in such habitats are still exposed to conditions that favor the evolution of a limited resistance to ammonia and nitrite.

The hardiness of most freshwater species exposed to substances such as ammonia and nitrite helps them survive the traumas of their first week or so in a newly set-up aquarium. Seawater aquarists, on the other hand, learned by trial and error that a newly set-up aquarium must be matured in accordance with proven techniques (see page 24) if massive losses due to ammonia poisoning are to be avoided. Because of this one peculiarity of marine organisms, seawater aquarists have learned to be more exacting and cautious than their freshwater counterparts. Indeed, the major advances in filtration technology in the last couple of decades have all come from this sphere of the hobby.

Every living thing produces waste products as a result of its metabolic processes. These waste products are broken down by bacteria into less harmful substances until the end product – nitrogen – is released as a gas into the atmosphere. The same process is carried out in the aquarium. All that is needed is a surface for the bacteria (*Nitrosomonas* and *Nitrobacter*) to colonize, a source of ammonia and a method of bringing the two together – the filter. There are many filtration methods and all do the same basic job, though in different ways. Before looking at the main methods, however, we should discuss the three main elements of filtration

Nitrogen cycle
A well-balanced nitrogen cycle is essential to a successful marine aquarium. Ammonia-based waste products are broken down into nitrites and then nitrates, which are either absorbed or removed during water changes.

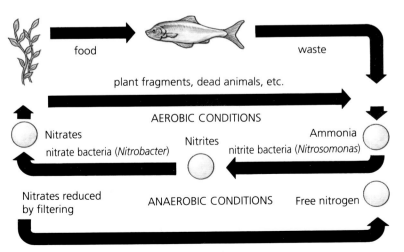

food   waste

plant fragments, dead animals, etc.

AEROBIC CONDITIONS

Nitrates   Ammonia

nitrate bacteria (*Nitrobacter*)   Nitrites   nitrite bacteria (*Nitrosomonas*)

Nitrates reduced by filtering   ANAEROBIC CONDITIONS   Free nitrogen

Reduction of nitrates by anaerobic denitrifying bacteria

Mechanical filtration, to put it simply, sieves the water to remove large particulate waste such as uneaten food and solid fish waste. The usual media used in mechanical filtration include sand and filter wool. Chemical filtration is a method whereby substances that biological filtration cannot deal with, including albumins, phenols and dyes, are removed from the system. Biological filtration makes use of bacteria, the part of the nitrogen cycle – known as nitrification – which is of most importance to the aquarist.

THE UNDERGRAVEL FILTER

This method is the most cost effective, the easiest to establish and therefore the most commonly used among beginner marine aquarists. The filter is simply a perforated plate that lies on the base of the aquarium. The plate is covered with a layer of a coarse medium such as coral gravel or crushed cockleshell. This layer is permeable to water but not to a second layer of finer medium on which the beneficial bacteria live and do their work. The ideal material for this layer is coral sand, which has the type of pores to allow it to be inundated with nitrifying bacteria. Both layers should be around 6–7.5 cm (2½–3 in) thick and it is a good idea to separate them with a piece of plastic mesh known as a gravel tidy. This simple device allows the free flow of water through the filter, but prevents the two media becoming mixed – something that will be appreciated should you need to strip the filter later.

Once the filter bed is in place, a method is needed to move the water through it in order to bring the waste products to the bacteria. To achieve this, the filter plate is fitted with one or more uplift tubes, which are just pipes that

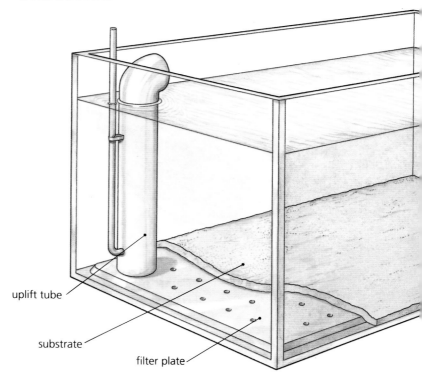

uplift tube

substrate

filter plate

carry water from under the filter bed back into the aquarium. Water is moved through the filter using powerheads. These are small, submersible pumps that sit on top of the uplift tubes. They are efficient, silent and some have the output being delivered calibrated on the side. In all but the smallest of aquariums it is preferable to use two uplifts, each with a powerhead that has the capacity to pump half of the total volume needed. As an example, we will take a small aquarium with a net capacity of, say, 135 liters (30 gal). For the filter to work at its optimum efficiency, three times that amount of water needs to move through it every hour, i.e. 135 x 3 = 405 liters (30 x 3 = 90 gal). Two pumps would be needed, each capable of moving 200 liters (45 gal) every hour. The use of two uplifts and pumps will ensure that there is an even distribution of water flowing through the filter at any one time.

Undergravel filter
A biological filter fitted underneath the substrate in an aquarium. Its perforated base is the first item placed in the tank.

REVERSE-FLOW
UNDERGRAVEL FILTERS

This method is merely an improvement on the previous one. One of the main drawbacks with conventional undergravel filtration is that the coral sand – being a very efficient mechanical filter – gets clogged very easily, preventing the filter from doing its job effectively. With the use of reverse-flow undergravel filtration, the water first goes to a canister filter for mechanical and, sometimes, chemical filtration. On leaving the canister filter, the water is then pumped down the uplift tube, under the filter bed and back into the main aquarium body of water. The advantage of this system is that the water has already been purged of large particulate waste before it comes into contact with the filter bed. In this way, the filter bed stays cleaner for longer periods of time, increasing the interval between cleanings (page 34).

Whichever method you choose, the bacteria in the filter, which are aerobic (needing high oxygen levels in order to survive), will compete with the fishes for the available oxygen in the aquarium. This will not create a problem as long as the aquarium is properly aerated. To achieve this, the powerhead outlets should be positioned as near as possible to the water surface in such a way as to create currents at the same time. To supplement this aeration, a high-output air pump can be used to supply large volumes of air to an air diffuser. The most efficient of these are made from limewood and produce a stream of tiny air bubbles, which are more efficient aerators. However, the main reason for aerating in this way is for the current it produces, which takes carbon dioxide from the bottom of the aquarium up to the water surface and circulates oxygen-laden water back down to the filter bed. Furthermore, the powerhead outlets provide another excellent way of breaking the water surface. If you choose reverse-flow undergravel filtration, it is essential to

Reverse-flow undergravel filter

The life of the filter will be extended considerably because water passes through a canister filter before reaching the filter bed.

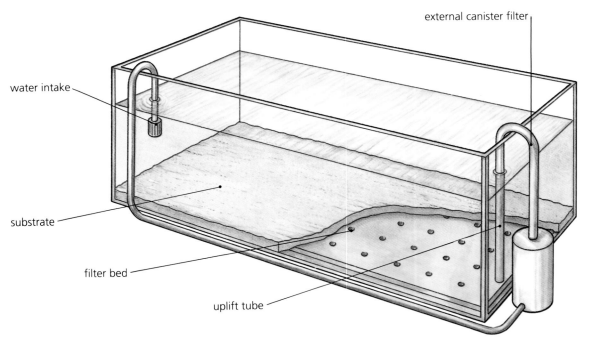

water intake

external canister filter

substrate

filter bed

uplift tube

aerate as fully as possible, since the water returning from the canister filter to the main tank is severely lacking in oxygen by the time it reaches its destination.

TRICKLE FILTRATION

This method of biological filtration – which has enjoyed a tremendous surge in popularity among serious aquarists over the past few years – scores heavily over the others because it takes the oxygen needed by the bacteria from the surrounding air, rather than from within the aquarium. Sometimes called wet-and-dry filtration, this method has the filter bed – usually porous clay granules and plastic media – sited either above or below the aquarium. Water that has first been cleaned of large particles of waste via a mechanical filter is then trickled over the filter granules, which, because of an unlimited supply of air, are able to multiply at a rate 20 times higher than in a conventional undergravel filter. Beneath these granules containing aerobic bacteria is another section of granules colonized by anaerobic bacteria because by the time the water has passed through the layer above, it is stripped of oxygen. These non-oxygen-loving bacteria set to work on the nitrates that are the by-product of the denitrification process carried out by the aerobic bacteria. They convert this nitrate to nitrous oxide and then, ultimately, to free nitrogen gas.

The third type of filtration, in addition to mechanical and biological, is chemical filtration, which removes the substances that the biological filter cannot handle. A seawater aquarium could be run moderately successfully without any chemical filtration at all. However, the substances, such as albumins, phenols and dyes, that are

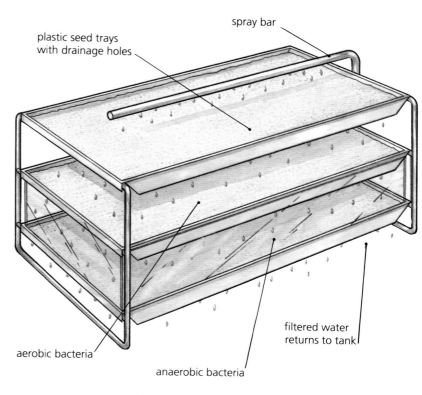

plastic seed trays with drainage holes

spray bar

aerobic bacteria

anaerobic bacteria

filtered water returns to tank

Trickle filter
This is a slow filter, which often involves inert granules, sand or an algal system.

filtered out with the following methods are almost non-existent in the wild. It makes sense, therefore, to eliminate them from the aquarium.

ACTIVATED CARBON

Activated carbon (charcoal) is an efficient way to remove dissolved organics from solution and is regularly used by experienced aquarists. It is able to do its job so well because each grain of carbon contains a myriad of microscopic pores that adsorb the substances and trap them there so that they are no longer in solution. The problem with activated carbon is that it will remove good things as well as bad, so it can be a mixed blessing. For instance, while it will remove organic waste such as phenols and dyes, it will also remove medications and other chemicals that may have been purposely added to the aquarium for the good of the fishes. Furthermore, the adsorption qualities of charcoal have only a limited lifespan and, when the pores in the charcoal have all been filled, all of the waste that has been adsorbed will be dumped back into the aquarium.

Activated carbon can be used in several ways, but the simplest method is to use a canister filter filled with a variety of media, one of them being charcoal. For example, a typical arrangement might be: filter sponge at the bottom of the canister, the charcoal – in a mesh bag – above it, a small amount of biological medium above that and at the top of the canister, some filter wool. The water enters at the top, runs through the filter wool first to remove any large particles, then over the biological media, then over the charcoal, before passing through the final layer of sponge on its way back into the aquarium. The best way to use activated carbon would be once a month for two or three days and then dispose of it, using new charcoal the next time.

There are charcoals designed for use in freshwater, as well as the type that is specifically for marine use. The freshwater charcoal is next to useless in the marine aquarium.

External biological filter

This is a highly efficient system. Water is filtered through a series of compartments filled with filtration medium (sand).

PROTEIN SKIMMING

Much of the organic waste that the biological filter cannot deal with – and much that it can – is material called surfactant. It is attracted to an air/water interface and is deposited when the interface breaks down. If a suitable air/water interface, such as a bubble, is provided and harnessed to collect the deposited organic material when the interface breaks down, waste can be removed from the aquarium completely. This is the basic principle of protein skimming, also called foam fractionating.

The simplest form of protein skimmer is a plastic column through which water and very fine air bubbles mix to form a surface foam. This is collected in a removable plastic cup. The resultant slime, which is composed of proteins, amino acids, albumins and other complex organic substances, is then easily collected and disposed of. Because the efficiency of protein skimmers depends on their height, the water flow rate and the amount of air that is supplied – which all dictate the amount of time the water is in contact with the air bubbles – more refined protein skimmers have appeared over the years. Counter-current skimmers, while still of the basic, air-driven variety, have the water driven down the tube from the top, against the flow of tiny air bubbles. This type of skimmer virtually doubles the water/air contact time available. Whichever type of air-driven unit you choose, be sure to buy the tallest unit available. Ensure that an efficient air pump is used and change the air diffuser every month to maintain the skimmer's efficiency.

A further development on the counter-current protein skimmer is the motor-driven, venturi type. With this

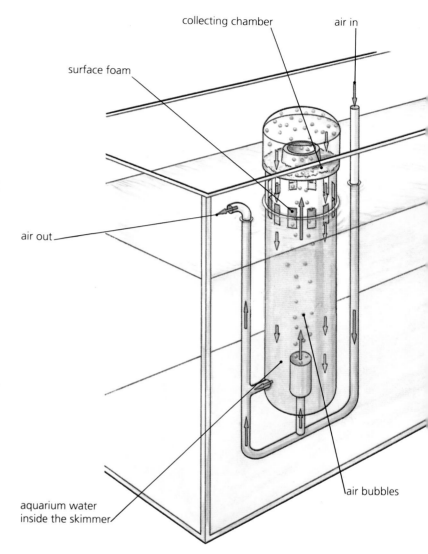

Protein skimmer
A simple device to remove proteins from the water by foaming. It can be air-driven or powered by electricity.

collecting chamber

air in

surface foam

air out

aquarium water inside the skimmer

air bubbles

type of skimmer, the water is pushed through, under pressure, by an electrical motor. Air is then introduced via a venturi, an air-intake mechanism that forces air into the water from the surroundings. This type of protein skimmer is much more expensive, but much more efficient.

Like activated carbon, a protein skimmer can remove desirable compounds such as medications. However, because skimmers can remove up to 80 percent of organics before they even reach the biological filter – thereby increasing the filter's effective life – and because of the substances they remove that the filter cannot, they are essential. You shouldn't contemplate running a seawater aquarium without one.

Ozone is produced by passing a supply of dried air over a high-voltage electrical charge, converting a proportion of the oxygen into ozone. Ozone gas is a very volatile oxidizing and disinfecting agent that can kill bacteria on contact. It also increases the efficiency of protein skimmers when it is added into the air supply of the skimmer. However, since ozone can only act upon free-swimming bacteria, and because there are so many problems inherent in its use in conjunction with a protein skimmer, its popularity has dwindled considerably and it is not recommended except for the more experienced hobbyist.

ULTRAVIOLET STERILIZERS
These units work by passing water that has already been mechanically filtered close to an ultraviolet light. The light can kill off bacteria, spores of algae and some parasites. However, because ultraviolet sterilizers, like ozonizers, can kill only free-swimming organisms and, – again like ozonizers – have limited uses, they are not entirely necessary for the beginner.

MATURING THE BIOLOGICAL FILTER

The most important part of the nitrogen cycle, as far as the aquarist is concerned, is the stage called nitrification, a step-by-step process by which harmful substances are broken down into less harmful ones, producing nitrogen gas as the end product. The bacteria involved – belonging to the genera *Nitrosomonas* and *Nitrobacter* – each produce the substance required as food by the next as a by-product of their activity.

Because the pH required in a seawater aquarium is very alkaline, the ammonia present is of the un-ionized variety, which is highly toxic when compared with ionized ammonia. The *Nitrosomonas* bacteria are the first to appear on the scene, quickly converting the ammonia to nitrite. *Nitrobacter* bacteria are inhibited by ammonia and will not appear until the ammonia level starts to fall. When this level does fall, the *Nitrobacter* start to convert the nitrite to nitrate. This nitrate is relatively harmless, but since fish do not encounter nitrate in the wild, it needs to be controlled in the aquarium. A trickle filter has provision for anaerobic bacteria to carry out this function. However, with an undergravel filter we have to control nitrates manually with partial water changes.

The biological filter is useless until a source of ammonia is provided to start the process. If an aquarium is stocked without first establishing a colony of beneficial bacteria through a process known as maturation, the result will be disastrous. The high levels of ammonia that would occur as the filter establishes itself would kill off the tank's inhabitants overnight. The temptation to stock a new marine aquarium with its full compliment of animals must be resisted, because impatience kills more marine organisms, and with it the hopes of the aquarist, than anything else.

In the past, the usual method of maturation was to add one or two hardy specimens, such as damselfishes. Their waste produced the initial source of ammonia needed to feed the nitrifying bacteria and start the process of bacteria multiplication, while their perceived tolerance of elevated ammonia levels would see them through the ordeal. This method is fraught with problems,

Damselfishes

The usual method of maturing the filter was to introduce one or two damselfishes. The modern way is by using maturation fluids, which are far more predictable.

however. We have already seen in earlier chapters that no species of coralfish can tolerate ammonia, and so this method is cruel in the extreme. Furthermore, as will be demonstrated later, the choice of species you choose to mature the filter will have a direct bearing on the species you will be able to select for your collection. It is much easier, more predictable and less cruel to use one of the commercially available maturation fluids. If the manufacturer's instructions are followed, maturation is usually achieved in a trauma-free manner within two or three weeks.

Maturation fluids are usually added to the aquarium on a daily basis and nitrite levels measured with a nitrite test kit after a period of time. The nitrite reading rises until a peak of around 15 parts per million (ppm) is reached, after which the levels of nitrite collapse to zero. By and large, once the nitrite level has remained at zero for one week, the filter can be considered mature. Because of all the activity that has gone on, however, the pH in the aquarium will have dipped considerably as a result. To combat this, a partial water change of 25% should be performed before any stock is added. Although an undergravel filter is very efficient, it cannot cope with the waste of an infinite number of fishes. It also needs time to adjust to the extra load created when a new fish is added to the tank. Stocking activities should therefore always be limited in accordance with the following rule: allow 2.5 cm (1 in) to every 18 liters (4 gal) of water for the first six months; then work up gradually to a maximum of 2.5 cm (1 in) of fish to every 9 liters (2 gal) thereafter. Fish length is measured from the tip of the snout to the base of the tail fin.

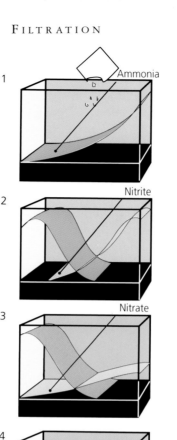
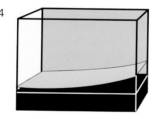
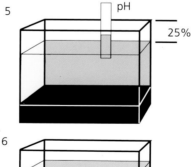
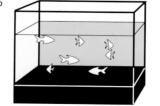

Maturing the biological filter

As a general rule, the filter can be considered mature once nitrite levels have remained at zero for a week. Perform partial water changes before introducing the fish into the tank.

1. Maturation compounds
added to start off nitrification. Ammonia levels peak.

2. Nitrosomonas bacteria convert ammonia to nitrite, the level of which then peaks.

3. Nitrobacter bacteria convert nitrites to nitrates.

4. Nitrates are reduced by water changes and nitrate filter (optional).

5. The pH level falls and a 25% water change is performed to counteract this.

6. Stock fishes are introduced gradually after further water changes.

WATER QUALITY AND TESTING

Far from needing a degree in chemistry, provided one is prepared to learn a few straightforward principles, there is no reason why a seawater aquarium shouldn't be trouble free.

Basically, water quality in the aquarium should replicate, as far as possible, that of the natural habitat. Of course, the aquarist has to monitor water quality regularly in order to know exactly what is going on in the aquarium at any given time. Test kits are available that provide all the information needed for maintaining the best possible environment for animals that, after all, have been taken from the wild. However, test kits are useless if you do not understand what they are telling you. Whether you use simple undergravel filtration (page 19), or whether you invest considerable sums of money in complete water management systems, the principles of water quality are the same.

NATURAL AND SYNTHETIC SEAWATER

Natural seawater is similar all over the world and provides such a stable habitat that one could be forgiven for thinking that it was the best medium for an aquarium. Not so. It may be true in the tropics, but seawater in temperate regions is much cooler than that from a coral reef and the planktonic animals within it are accustomed to those temperatures. The raised temperatures of a tropical aquarium would either kill them outright or stimulate them to reproduce at an uncontrollable rate. Either way, this could cause untold damage. Before natural seawater is used in an aquarium, it must be stored in total darkness for months, until all the planktonic organisms are dead, and this is out of the question for most people.

The composition of seawater around the world is, essentially, the same: 55% chlorine, 30.5% sodium, 7.5% sulphate, 3.5% magnesium, 1% each of calcium, potassium and trace elements, and 0.5% bicarbonate. Modern synthetic seawater

Hydrometers

The modern "swing-needle" type hydrometer attached to this tank is easier to use and more accurate than the older types. Older examples must be used with a phial, and the s.g. must be calculated with account taken of the water temperature.

is so good that there are very few brands that do not contain all of the elements required for the well-being of marine life. In fact, one or two contain beneficial components in greater quantities than the real thing. With all the inherent problems that the use of natural seawater could present, there is no valid reason for not using synthetic.

MEASURING SALINITY

As stated earlier, the most straightforward way to measure salinity is by measuring the density, or specific gravity, of the water (see page 11). There are other, more technical ways of measuring salinity, but most aquarists talk about specific gravity, commonly called S.G. The device used to measure S.G. is called a hydrometer, and can be bought from any aquarium store.

Hydrometers come in two forms. The first is a basic, traditional floating hydrometer of the type regularly used by brewers. With this type of hydrometer, water from the aquarium is taken into a phial and then the hydrometer dropped into it. The S.G. is read off at the water line. Don't use this unit in the aquarium itself because the currents in the tank will prevent you from getting an accurate reading. Make sure, also, that you only use one specially designed for use in marine aquariums — never a brewer's model. A second — and the far superior — type is the modern swing-needle hydrometer. Just fill the container with aquarium water and read the S.G. from the gauge printed on the side, indicated by a swing-needle. The old-fashioned hydrometers are calibrated to measure at 24°C (75°F) and the user must calculate the S.G. at different temperatures, but the swing-needle type gives accurate readings whatever the water temperature.

Specific gravity may fluctuate in the aquarium for a number of reasons. However, the most common reason for fluctuations in S.G. is evaporation. Evaporation occurs from any body of water over a period of time, the rate of evaporation being governed by temperature and currents. An aquarium is no exception, but a seawater aquarium does have one peculiarity. When seawater evaporates, the salts dissolved within it stay where they are. This has the effect of raising salinity, as the proportion of salt to water increases.

As the object is to keep every aspect of the aquarium — including salinity — stable, the imbalance caused by evaporation needs to be rectified. Specific gravity needs to be checked regularly and evaporation loss made up with fresh water. It is advisable to check S.G. every two or three days, so that evaporation is rectified in small stages. Should this be neglected — and S.G. rise by more than one point — the increase in salinity can cause untold stress in the fishes. Finally, it should be remembered that any deliberate change in salinity must be made gradually.

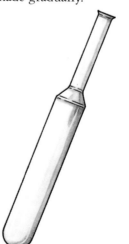

Hydrometers
This older-type hydrometer is cheap and widely available, but account must be taken of the water temperature.

pH IN THE AQUARIUM

The pH (level of acidity or alkalinity) of natural seawater is fairly constant within any given area, whether it is the open ocean or on a coral reef. Another characteristic of seawater is its high pH, meaning that it is alkaline. This high alkalinity must be replicated in the aquarium, within a range of 8.0 to 8.3. A level below that is getting hazardously low and one above that will result in excess toxic ammonia. You must also ensure that, whatever the pH of the aquarium water within the above range, it remains constant. Remember that pH is measured on a logorithmic scale, meaning that each point is ten times greater or lower than the one before. A shift in pH from 8.1 to 8.2, for example, means that the pH has risen ten times. Fortunately, there are two significant points that help to maintain the pH level. First, synthetic seawater has a tremendous buffering capacity. This means that it is capable of maintaining the correct pH in spite of all the activities going on within the aquarium. Second, provided that all the rules regarding feeding, stocking and water changes are adhered to, the pH of your aquarium will take care of itself. Fish waste and uneaten food lying around in the tank will lower the pH level, so great care must be taken not to have too many fishes, too much food or too few water changes – the most efficient method of raising pH – in the aquarium.

Serious aquarists, especially those involved with sensitive coral invertebrates, now use electronic equipment to test pH, but the most cost-effective means of monitoring pH is with a test kit, using either liquid or powder reagents. A small amount of aquarium water is taken in a phial supplied with the kit. A quantity of the reagent is then added to the water

pH test kits

To test for pH, add the required amount of reagent to a sample of the aquarium water and shake to mix. Now match the color of the mixture to the printed and calibrated color charts.

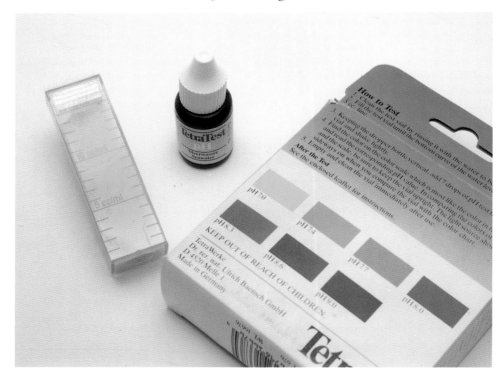

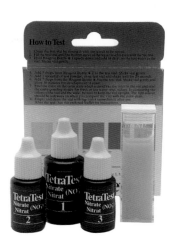

sample and a short period of time allowed to elapse, after which the color of the water in the phial will have changed. It is then a simple matter to compare the color of the water with the color chart supplied. Provided that the reading is within the required range, all is well. If the pH has dropped since the last test, this should be rectified with either a partial water change (best) or by using a proprietory pH adjuster. Sodium bicarbonate can be used with equally speedy results. A word of warning, however: these pH adjusters only plaster over the cracks. If pH is a problem, the whole aquarium system should be checked for any failings, such as overstocking, overfeeding, dirty filters or poor water circulation. Furthermore, the effects of pH adjusters can be drastic, so they should never be used to adjust pH by more than one point at a time. The effects of using sodium bicarbonate are usually temporary, so it shouldn't be relied on for anything other than a "quick-fix".

A few warnings on test kits are in order here. First, those with liquid reagents can have a far shorter life than those containing reagents in solid form. Test kits that have exceeded their shelf-life will give inaccurate readings. Second, the color charts that come with these kits should always be kept in a dark place as light will cause the colors to fade, which, again, will lead to incorrect readings. Finally, it should be remembered that the reagents contained within these kits are poisonous. Always store them carefully, out of reach of children and animals. Always wash your hands thoroughly after using test kits.

Water quality in relation to ammonia, nitrite and nitrate has already been discussed, but these must also be monitored. Test kits for these substances all work on the same basic principle. They involve taking a water sample, adding reagents and then comparing the resultant color change against a color chart. In the earlier stages, an ammonia test kit can be dispensed with, but a nitrite test kit is essential for monitoring the maturation process. This can be followed by a nitrate kit once the filter is matured, and then an ammonia test kit if you are interested in gaining the full picture of your aquarium's water chemistry.

Test kits

The successful marine aquarist will have a range of test kits at his or her disposal. Although serious experienced hobbyists now use electronic monitoring systems, liquid or powder test kits are more cost effective.

SETTING UP A MARINE AQUARIUM

Up to this point, we have dealt with fairly technical information, but now we can discuss something far more exciting – the setting-up of an aquarium. The first aspect of the aquarium that has to be considered is decoration. After reading thus far, you could be forgiven for thinking that a bare tank would make life easier with regard to keeping everything clean. However, decoration in the form of rocks, coral skeletons and so on, is important for two reasons. A bare tank looks very stark and has no aesthetic value. Secondly, many fish species live either in or very close to caves and similar crevices. To sentence them to an unnatural way of life would be folly, imposing great stress upon them, and stress is the biggest killer of coralfishes.

ROCKWORK AND DECORATION

There are many types of decoration available to the marine hobbyist, including rocks, coral skeletons, shells and novelty "toys", some of which are air-operated. However, considering the incredible natural beauty of coralfishes, it would be gilding the lily to introduce garish castles or dispeptic divers.

Basically, any type of rock that does not contain metallic streaks or chemicals

Tank decorations
Rockwork and other decorations play an important role in the aquarium environment. Not only do they make the tank look attractive, but they also provide diversions and safe havens for the fish.

such as sulfur, or is of an acidic nature, can be used in the marine aquarium. Slate can be attractive and could be used, but it is very heavy and displaces a lot of water compared to its bulk. Rocks and pebbles picked from the beach would probably be safe, but they would pose the same problem. As much space as possible needs to be kept for fish, not for rocks.

The best rocks to use are either man-made lava rock, or tufa. The lava rock has many advantages over all other types. Chief among these is the fact that it displaces very little water. In addition, it varies so much in color that, when under water, it looks for all the world like the natural "living" rock of the coral reef. It is also very easy to stack into an interesting seascape. However, its edges can be sharp, so handle it with care. Lava rock is expensive, but is the best type for the seawater aquarium. One word of warning: this rock should never be confused with natural volcanic lava, which is high in sulfur and must never be used.

Tufa, on the other hand, is a naturally occurring rock that is almost entirely calcium. It has all the chemical properties of coral sand and, like coral sand, has a beneficial buffering effect upon the aquarium's pH. Tufa is also very soft and can be gouged and shaped to the aquarist's taste or requirements. Like man-made lava rock, it is also acceptable from the point of view of water displacement, since it is extremely porous. Tufa does have a slight disadvantage in that it is very light in color and can appear very stark at first. However, a couple of weeks in the aquarium will see it becoming encrusted with algae and this brightness will disappear. On the whole, tufa can be especially recommended.

CORAL SKELETONS

The coral on sale in aquarium stores is actually the skeletons of the dead polyps that have built up over many years. These coral skeletons come in all shapes and sizes – and three different colors. However, it is now illegal for many countries to export coral skeletons for conservation reasons and environmentalists may wish to use synthetic corals. These are made by molding inert resins, usually by the people who once collected real coral. These synthetic corals are available in the same range of the shapes and sizes as the real thing, cost no more and the aquarist has the satisfaction of knowing that he or she has not contributed to destruction.

Before coral skeletons can be used in an aquarium, you must ensure that they do not carry any remains of the coral polyps that once lived on them. It was advocated that coral be immersed in household bleach for a week, then washed and immersed in several changes of fresh water for at least another week. This is now considered unnecessary, and coral skeletons are only treated this way when pieces of coral are too big to be boiled. Nowadays, coral skeletons are usually boiled for at least half an hour and then rinsed in clean, fresh water.

SHELLS

Shells, in all their various forms and colors – especially the large attractive ones such as conch shells, add a third, natural dimension to the aquarium scene. Large shells also have enough space inside to provide refuge for some of the smaller species of fish. Shells also need to be cleaned of any dead animal matter by boiling for half an hour and then rinsing in cold water.

Decorations
An assortment of rocks, coral skeletons and shells suitable for the marine tank.

SETTING UP

When all the decorations are ready, the tank with an undergravel filter can be set up. Make sure that you plan this operation down to the finest detail, as time spent on this stage will mean time saved later. Make sure that the area around the aquarium site is clear of everything not required for the job as you will not want to be injured falling over a stool while carrying the aquarium. When all this is done, the tank can be washed with clean water – not soap and water – and placed on its stand. To iron out any imperfections in either the tank or the stand, which would cause stress on the aquarium and probably crack it, you could place polystyrene tiles or a piece of carpet on the stand before the tank is set down.

Once the aquarium is in place, lay the filter plate on the base of the tank. In large aquariums, two or more filter plates must be used, cut to fit. Once these are in place, fit the uplift tubes into the plates, making sure that they are securely in position. Next comes the coral gravel or cockleshell that is to form the basis of the filter bed. Obviously, the larger the tank, the more filter material will be needed. More than one bucketful will be required.

It is now time to lay the gravel-tidy. Cut this to size, and cut out the holes for the uplifts, trying not to leave too many gaps or the two filter media will mix. Wash the coral sand in the same way as the coral gravel, and lay that over everything else. Some authorities suggest sloping the sand from front to back so that all debris rolls to the front for ease of cleaning. In practice, this doesn't work, as the sand will find its own level once the water is poured in. However, care should be taken to get an even spread. At this point the powerheads can be positioned and the heaters installed. Then install the lights, but on no account must the electrical equipment be turned on at this stage. The heaters should go in a semi-vertical position where they will get a good flow of water around them. Never place a heater flat on the sand.

At this point, the rocks can be laid out according to your own sense of design. Once everything is in place, the aquarium can be filled with water. A 22.5 liter (5 gal) bucket is best for this because you can measure exactly how much water the aquarium holds while filling it, making accurate dosing of treatments easy. Keeping a note of every bucketful, fill the aquarium to the point where the water level is hidden by the (black) trim at the top of the tank. The electrical equipment can now be switched on and the aquarium left overnight. In the morning, everything should be working correctly and the water should have reached the temperature that you preset on the thermostat. It is now a simple matter to add the salt. If you monitored exactly how much water went into the tank, you can make a straightforward calculation to ascertain how much salt to add. A rough guide – based on a specific gravity of 1.020 – is that 1 kg (2 lb) of salt will give 30 liters (7 gal) of seawater. Add the salt gradually over a period of one or two hours, then wait another 24 hours to allow all the salt to dissolve fully and check the specific gravity. If it is too low, add more salt. If it is too high, draw off some water, lay it aside for future use, then add more fresh water. After a wait of a further day or two, the maturation process can begin (see page 24).

Setting up the tank

1. First, place the perforated baseplates of a biological or undergravel filter (see page 19) on the bottom of the tank.

2. Locate the airlift tube securely in position at the corner of the tank, being careful not to break it, especially near the baseplate.

3. Next, wash the gravel that is to form the base of the filter bed and spread it evenly over the filter plates. For your marine aquarium, you should then lay the gravel-tidy in place and cover everything with a layer of rinsed coral sand.

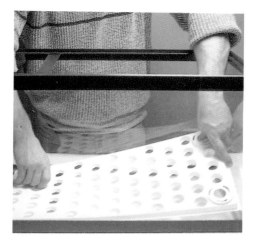

4. Now you can install the heaters. Before switching them on, remember to raise them above the bed of the aquarium. They can be attached to the side of the tank with rubber suckers.

5. Position the powerheads on the uplift tubes, being careful to secure any trailing wires.

6. As for a freshwater aquarium, you should next add some decorations. Rocks and coral are best for a marine environment. Finally, lay a plate or dish on the sand to prevent distribution and fill the aquarium with water from a bucket to monitor the capacity.

REGULAR MAINTENANCE

Unfortunately, it is not enough to set up an aquarium properly and to buy and introduce fishes carefully. The whole system needs to be maintained regularly if the fish are to remain happy. There is no magic formula for those wonderful aquariums, with their healthy and happy fishes. The only way to achieve such a sight on a long-term basis is by regular maintenance.

The first step is to become used to checking the aquarium every time you feed the fishes. There is very probably no time to do this in the mayhem that is part of the average household morning, so it should be done at the evening feed. Check that everything is working as it should. Check the temperature, make sure that all the pumps are performing and check to see whether the protein skimmer needs emptying. Also, watch the fishes and make sure that they are all present and behaving as they should.

It cannot be stressed enough how important it is that you get to know your aquarium and its inhabitants inside out. To this end, many of the best aquarists keep a log of their tanks, in which they record everything they do and everything they add. The dates of these events should be included and its not a bad idea to monitor and record the results. Only by being methodical can you truly get to know your aquarium, thereby enjoying it to the full and spotting signs of trouble quickly. The following table lists all the regular tasks and how often to perform them. If this looks like too much trouble, maybe you should think again about the whole venture. All the jobs put together only account for a few minutes every day and an hour or two on the weekend. It should also be pointed out that neglecting these small maintenance tasks will lead to a lot of work sooner or later.

WATER CHANGES

The 22.5 liter (5 gal) bucket has been mentioned before, but it is a good idea

MAINTENANCE PROGRAM

Every day
Check the temperature.
Check that the fishes are all present and behaving normally.
Empty the protein skimmer cup if necessary.
Make sure that all the equipment is functioning correctly.
Remove uneaten food.

Every other day
Top up the aquarium to replace evaporated water. Remove unwanted algae from the front glass with an algae magnet.

Every week
Clean the cover glasses of salt residue and algae, which hamper light efficiency.
Perform all the other tasks mentioned above.
Change 10% of the water in the aquarium. This will be far easier than changing large amounts every month (see above).
Measure ammonia, nitrite, nitrate and pH levels with the appropriate test kits (see page 28).
Replace filter wool in canister filter if necessary.
Harvest unwanted algae.

to buy at least two, for this use only. They are useful for so many tasks that you will find there are times when one bucket just will not be enough.

The day before water-change day, mix the salt with fresh water from the faucet in the bucket. It does not matter that you need, for example 36 liters (8 gal) of water and the bucket holds only 22.5 liters (5 gal). The extra water can be added the following day. Using a small air pump, a length of airline and an airstone, aerate the water overnight. Faucet water contains chlorine and aeration will drive it off, but a commercial dechlorinator will be needed to deal with chloramines. If you possess a spare heater, this can be used to bring the new water to the same temperature as the aquarium. When you change the water, check the S.G. and adjust with more water or salt as needed. Check the temperature and adjust with boiled water if necessary. This doesn't have to be too exact provided that you either add the new water slowly or have a large

tank where a small amount of cooler water will not be noticed.

On water-change day, first rake through the filter bed. It is best to use your hands for this so that you can feel for any clogging and eliminate it. This raking will result in a cloud of mulm (layer of detritus), which will quickly settle back onto the sand. Using a siphon tube – a wide bore tube available from any aquarium store – siphon off the mulm with the required amount of water. Don't worry if you don't get all the mulm out. Any that is left behind can be removed next time. It is now a simple matter to add the new water slowly and replace the newly cleaned cover glasses.

Siphoning
Use a siphon or siphon pump to remove water from the tank with as little disruption as possible. Hold one end of the tube just above the gravel bed, with the other end leading to a bucket.

Every month
Replace air diffusers, including the one in the protein skimmer.
Check all electrical wiring.
Clean the protein skimmer. If an air-operated skimmer is used, clean the whole unit in hot water. This will eradicate any grease and albumin, which hamper its operation. With a power skimmer of the venturi type, only the cup will need cleaning in this way.
Clean out any canister filters, washing the biological medium in tank water only.
Clean light reflectors, if used.

As required
Replace lighting tubes.
Clean pumps as instructed by the makers. Air pumps contain a diaphram, which needs to be replaced on a regular basis if the pump is to maintain its efficiency.

Buying fish and introducing them into the tank

You have a much better chance of maintaining an aquarium of happy, healthy fishes if you start with healthy stock. Fish carry so many pathogens – the organisms that cause disease – that it only takes a period of stress to give the pathogens a foothold and make the animal sick. There is no foolproof way of making sure that the fishes you buy are 100% healthy, but these are some helpful guidelines.

It is important to remember that, with very few exceptions, the fishes and invertebrates in a dealer's store have come from the wild. If the cost of coralfishes comes as a surprise, bear in mind all the costs involved in the process of catching them, freight and, of course, holding them at the wholesalers/importers. Add to this the amount lost by all parties in the process due to mortalities, and the cost of distribution once they get to the destination country, and it is easy to see where your money is going. Secondly, given all of the stages in the process that the fish has had to endure, it has been through a very stressful time. All of this should be kept in mind when choosing coralfishes for the aquarium.

FINDING A DEALER

While your aquarium's filter system is maturing, use the two or three weeks to visit all the aquarium stores in your area. Talk to the permanent workers in the store, who should be knowledgable on the subject. Remember, however, that this may be difficult at busy times. Some of the best aquatic dealers are small, one-man operations, and it is not unreasonable for such a dealer to expect some payment for his advice and time.

Your chosen dealer should be committed to selling healthy fishes and invertebrates. It should be a specialist aquarium store, not a pet store with just a tank or two at the back. The store should be clean and well run, with a good selection not only of livestock, but equipment too. Most importantly, the dealer should be prepared to tell you the name of his suppliers. Finally, when you have found a dealer, stick with him. Dealers are much more likely to go out of their way to help a regular, long-standing customer and to search for that fish that you have set your heart on.

Fish care

When keeping herbivores, like these Regal Tangs, a regular feed of lettuce will provide a good substitute if the tank lacks a natural growth of algae.

SPOTTING HEALTHY SPECIMENS

When buying fish, it pays to be a good observer. Be patient! Don't buy the first creature you see simply because it is on your list.

You will sometimes see fishes that are wasting away – with areas of pinching around the stomach area or, more commonly, behind the eyes, as though someone had taken the fish's head between their thumb and first finger and squeezed. These are signs of trouble and you should leave the fish where it is. Having said that, surgeons and tangs (and other species that live exclusively on a diet of algae) are probably merely suffering the effects of being deprived of their natural diet for a few days. Return to the store a few days later and you could see a quite different beast. Always check for any dead or dying animals in the aquarium. Even if the fish you have your eye on appears to be healthy, if one or more of its tankmates is about to die,

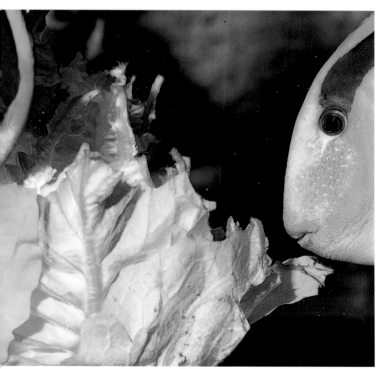

walk away. There is a problem in that aquarium, and it will almost certainly manifest itself in your purchase as soon as you get it home.

Make sure that all the fishes in the aquarium are swimming around and behaving normally. Here again, there is a proviso. You should never buy a fish without first doing some homework on the species because you need to know what is "normal" for any species. For instance, some species do swim in a strange way, and others hide for most of the time. Make sure that all fishes in the aquarium are displaying their normal colorations. If you are unsure whether this is the case, again leave it and do some reading. At the very least, ask the dealer about it. It could be that, two minutes before you walked into the store, there was an almighty scuffle in the tank and the species is one of those that displays its anger or fright by changing color. However, it could well mean something is wrong with the fish.

Finally, it is essential to ascertain whether or not a fish is feeding and what it is feeding on. Some authorities suggest asking to see the fish feed. However, this is foolish. If you watch the beast consume a large meal, you will probably be impressed enough to buy it. However, the fish is likely to excrete its food into the bag that you take it home in, polluting the water and probably killing itself. Simply ask the dealer if the fish you are interested in is feeding, and decide whether you trust the dealer.

You must ascertain the feeding status of any fish before you buy it. Only then can you make an informed decision. While asking the question, find out also what the animal eats. Then, at least, you will have a chance of successfully introducing it into your aquarium.

INTRODUCING FISHES INTO THE AQUARIUM

Whether you run a quarantine aquarium or not, fishes must be introduced into their new home in the most stress-free way possible. The most common advice is to float the plastic bag in which the fish was brought home in the aquarium for an hour or so, gradually equalizing temperature and water conditions, before releasing the fish. However, this process is fraught with problems. All the fish already in the aquarium will come to investigate what is going on, thereby stressing the newcomer. Also, the sides of plastic bags have a tendency to collapse, making the bag fold in on itself, stressing the fish even further.

By far the best way to introduce a newcomer is to use a small, plastic aquarium such as one sold for goldfish. Simply tip the contents of the bag, including the fish, into this as carefully as possible and allow the animal a few moments to orientate itself. While it is doing this, turn off the lights in the main aquarium so that the other fishes quiet down and, with luck, go to ground. Gradually, over a period of an hour at least, introduce water from the main aquarium into the small tank. Check the salinity in both aquariums with a hydrometer and, when they are identical, carefully pick the fish out of the small tank using your hands or a container if the fish has sharp or venomous spines, not a net – nets can cause damage – and put it into the aquarium, opening your hands and waiting until the fish swims away. Leave the lights off in the aquarium until the next morning and the fish should be swimming around looking for food.

COMPATIBILITY IN THE AQUARIUM

When choosing fishes for an aquarium collection, the main criteria to be taken into account are the behavioral idiosyncracies of different species. The beginner first has to learn all he or she can about a given family or species before making the first purchase. Advice is given on this in the Species Directory (from page 40), although there is no reason why individual fish should conform to type.

The most obvious factor is whether one species is likely to prey on another in the aquarium. Some species, such as lionfishes and groupers, are very predatory and will have no compunction about eating anything that will fit into their huge mouths. Obviously, therefore, it would be foolish to house them with small damselfishes. Predatory species are clearly indicated in the directory.

The facet of life that most affects the ability of fishes to live together is territory. There are two ways in which fishes display territorial behavior. First, a species will fight off any member of the same or a similar species competing against it for food. Furthermore, there are species that will fight off even totally dissimilar species if they perceive them as a threat to the food supply. Many species will defend a cave or similar hiding place where it spends the night or in which it retreats in the face of danger. While these species will ignore others away from their shelter, they will attack violently when near to it. This form of aggression is usually very easily managed.

The final type of aggressive behavior to take into account is that shown by a parent guarding either a nest site or offspring. Again, this is usually managed without too much trouble.

For these reasons the aquarist must learn all they can about their prospective purchase, although it should be

Dried foods

There is a variety of dried foods available from suppliers, including tablet forms, different sized flakes and freeze-dried krill. Use them with other types of food for a balanced diet.

remembered that many coral species are not at all territorial, and many do far better when kept in the company of others of the same species than when kept as single specimens.

FEEDING

The species directory contains advice on the natural diets of individual species and what to feed them in the aquarium. However, there are one or two rules to observe when feeding.

Never overfeed your fishes. One old rule was to feed only enough food to cover a fish's eye, for each fish in the aquarium. A more modern pointer is to feed only as much food as can be consumed in a few minutes. Anything left uneaten after this time should be removed. Fishes also do much better if fed little and often. With the exception of predators such as lionfishes, which should only be fed every other day, as in nature, fishes should be fed at least twice a day. A meal of flake food in the morning and one of frozen or live food in the evening is about right.

Fresh and frozen foods

These types of food provide the main diet for many marine species. Thaw out frozen foods in suitable portions as required. These foods can include lancefish, mussels and shrimps. These foods are convenient to use, but don't forget that some species also require live food at times.

SECTION FOUR
DIRECTORY OF FISH SPECIES
and their care

ACANTHURIDAE

SURGEONFISHES *and* TANGS

The surgeonfish family is among the most popular groups with marine aquarists. Indeed, it would be difficult to find devotees who have not kept a surgeonfish at some time during their seawater-aquarium career. Surgeonfish get their name from the erectile spines, which look very much like scalpels, positioned on each side of the body just in front of the caudal peduncle. Some Surgeons expose their scalpels for all to see, but the majority keep them hidden in a kind of sheath. When they are fighting they flick out the spines and with a swish of the tail can cause serious – sometimes mortal – damage to an adversary. This may give the impression that they are a vicious family. However, while it's true that some species are aggressive, they are not all like that. With a little knowledge of what other species can be kept with them, even the most aggressive specimens can be kept successfully. Having said this, they can all hold their own against a bully.

The Acanthurids are found in tropical seas all over the world, although they are not well represented in the tropical Atlantic. Like the majority of marine aquarium fish, they are most common in the Indo-Pacific. They are deep-bodied, laterally compressed fish with brilliant colors and patterns. They usually have small mouths and fine, chisel-like teeth with which they scrape algae from rocks and corals. Some are also blessed with thick-walled, rasping stomachs which,

presumably, help them to deal with algae, their natural food.

If surgeonfishes and tangs are to stay healthy in the aquarium, their natural diet must be replicated If there is a good growth of algae within the tank, so much the better. If not, a substitute must be provided. Blanched lettuce is probably the easiest to offer and is certainly the best received. Buy the soft-leaved, round lettuce, as surgeons can't

Q I would love to keep a surgeon species, but have no algae in my aquarium to speak of. What can I do?

A You say you have no algae "to speak of." Well, as long as it is green, the algae you have will probably be enough to satisfy one tang specimen. However, feed lettuce or spinach at least twice a week to supplement it.

Acanthuridae
This is one of the most popular families in the hobby. The species get their popular name from the scalpel-like spines on either side of their caudal peduncle.

digest the coarser types, and prepare it by pouring boiling water over it to break down the cellulose. To feed the lettuce to the fish you can either buy lettuce clips that hold it in place, or place it between the two halves of an algae magnet and drop it to the bottom of the aquarium. Be sure to take it out when the fish have stopped feeding; there is no point in risking pollution. Other substitutes for algae are thawed-out frozen peas and spinach. Treat the latter like lettuce if not frozen.

ACANTHURUS ACHILLES

ACHILLES TANG

This Pacific Ocean species, with its dark brown body and orange spot on the caudal peduncle, near the tail, makes a very striking addition to an aquarium. The orange spot hides this species' scalpel, as well as giving rise to its popular name. It lives on the crests of coral reefs, where there is a lot of water turbulence, and to keep it in the best of health in an aquarium you need to make sure that there is plenty of water movement. If you can provide this, and plenty of algae, there is no reason why species members shouldn't live for years. This species either does well in captivity or dies very quickly, so make sure that you buy a specimen that has had time to adjust to the regime of aquarium life at your supplier. If you see one you like, put down a deposit, and wait a week or two before you pay the balance and take it home. That way you know that it has settled in and started feeding at your supplier.

Acanthurus achilles
Maybe not the easiest to keep but certainly the most handsome of the tangs.

Acanthurus leucosternon
A good water quality indicator, this species becomes very pallid if conditions are lacking.

ACANTHURUS LEUCOSTERNON

POWDER BLUE SURGEON

This species is found primarily in the Indian Ocean and has been recorded from Mauritius in the west to Sri Lanka in the east. Although a handsome species, it is very aggressive. It should always be the last fish that you add to your collection, and even then it may cause trouble. It should never be trusted with either small fishes or invertebrates. It feeds heavily on algae, but small protein foods should be offered regularly. It is very sensitive to water quality and will turn pale when something is amiss. It will also do this, however, when it is in an angry or aggressive mood.

KEY

LENGTH IN WILD (IN)

LENGTH IN CAPTIVITY (IN)

HERBIVORE

OMNIVORE

PREDATOR

SINGLE SPECIMEN

COMMUNITY FISH

SAFE WITH SMALL FISHES

SAFE WITH INVERTEBRATES

EASE OF KEEPING FOR BEGINNERS (SCALE OF 1–10) **7**

ACANTHURUS GLAUCOPAREIUS

GOLD-RIMMED SURGEON

Acanthurus glaucopareius
Like its cousin, *A. achilles*, this species needs perfect water quality for good health.

This species comes from the Pacific and can also be found in the Indian Ocean. Some aquarists call it the Powder-brown Surgeon and a quick comparison with *A. leucosternon* shows why. Apart from their appearance, however, there are few similarities between them. They both feed primarily on algae, but while *A. leucosternon* also feeds on small animals such as worms and shrimps, this species does not appear to. It is also generally peaceful, although it shouldn't be trusted with invertebrates such as tubeworms or with anemones and corals. Its favorite haunts in the wild are surge channels where the water is invariably white and bubbly, so good aeration and water movement is vital for its health in the aquarium.

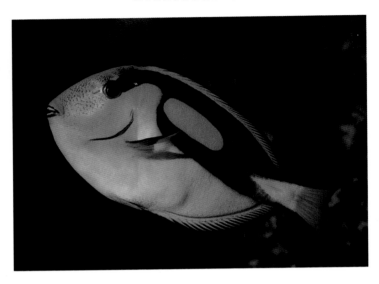

Paracanthurus hepatus

Who could argue that this species is indeed the "bluest thing on Earth"?

PARACANTHURUS HEPATUS

REGAL TANG

*F*ound in the Indo-Pacific, this species has been called "the bluest thing on Earth." The deep blue of its body, the curved black pattern on its flank, set off with a bright yellow tail, make this one of the most striking of all coral reef fishes. Although it is a very peaceful species, individuals tend to fight amongst themselves in the aquarium, so it should be kept as a single specimen. It can be kept with invertebrates, although caution should be a watchword, and smaller fishes in the same tank will not be in danger. Although a vegetarian most of the time, like *Acanthurus glaucopareius,* it will also feed on things like brine shrimps if given the chance.

ZEBRASOMA FLAVESCENS

YELLOW TANG

*H*ailing from Hawaii, this tang can be kept with others of the same species provided that the aquarium is large enough for a group of six or so. If this is not the case, it must be kept as a single specimen. The Yellow Tang is highly territorial and two individuals in a small area would tear each other apart. Do not be fooled by dealers' tanks, which may well house two or three. Fish never show their true nature at the dealers, for reasons looked at earlier (see pages 36–37).

Zebrasoma flavescens

One of the few species in the hobby which has an unbroken, solid colour.

Zebrasoma veliferum
Commonly referred to as peaceful, this species can actually be very vicious at times.

KEY

LENGTH IN WILD (IN)	
LENGTH IN CAPTIVITY (IN)	
HERBIVORE	
OMNIVORE	
PREDATOR	
SINGLE SPECIMEN	
COMMUNITY FISH	
SAFE WITH SMALL FISHES	
SAFE WITH INVERTEBRATES	
EASE OF KEEPING FOR BEGINNERS (SCALE OF 1–10)	

ZEBRASOMA VELIFERUM

SAILFIN TANG

*F*ound in the Indo-Pacific and, less commonly, the Red Sea, this species' common name comes from its huge dorsal fin, which seems to shrink in proportion to its overall size as the fish matures. Although it is often described as a peaceful fish, experience has shown that the Sailfin Tang can be rather nasty. It tends to ignore small fishes, but should never be kept with invertebrates or with other Sailfin Tangs. This is another tang which eats other things as well as algae.

Q I cannot decide whether to keep a Yellow Tang or a Regal Tang. I already have a Clownfish with anemone, a Bicolor angel and a Bicolor Blenny.

A Either will be fine with the specimens you already have. However, the Yellow Tang looks at its best when in a group, so the Regal Tang is probably best for you.

APOGONIDAE

CARDINALFISHES

This fairly large family is found in shallow, tropical seas, although some species inhabit deeper waters in temperate regions. And some cardinalfishes are freshwater species. Only two species are of any importance to the aquarium hobbyist – *Apogon maculatus* and *Sphaeramia nematopterus*. Most members of the family are found in the Indo-Pacific, where they spawn on reef areas. The cardinalfishes are mainly nocturnal, spending the daylight hours hiding in crevices, caves and among coral heads and becoming very active at night.

These very colorful little fishes have two dorsal fins, each with only two spines. Cardinalfishes also have large heads, mouths and eyes – features that characterize both this family and nocturnal species in general. In many tropical cardinalfish species the males incubate the eggs in their mouths and can be distinguished from the females by their deeper, wider head shape.

Although these species will need time to acclimatize to aquarium conditions, once they have, they are very hardy and will eat almost anything, although some authorities claim that they will not eat flake foods. Because they are nocturnal, it is a good idea to feed these fishes in semidarkness. This will allow them to feed as they would in the wild. The cardinalfishes make an excellent beginner's choice, and are superb additions to an invertebrate aquarium.

Apogonidae
A group of small, shallow-water fishes, which make excellent additions to an invertebrate aquarium.

APOGON MACULATUS

FLAMEFISH

This is a common species in the western Atlantic, from Bermuda in the north down to Brazil in the south, and throughout the Caribbean. It is seen from just below the shoreline down to depths of around 130 m (430 ft). It can be recognized from its bright red coloration, with thin white lines running above and below the eye, and black patches under the second dorsal fin and on the caudal peduncle (although the latter can be very faint). The flamefish makes an excellent addition to the aquarium provided that no boisterous species is kept with it, as it is somewhat shy. It likes to eat small creatures such as brine shrimps and bloodworms, although it will also relish larger food if it is chopped small enough to fit into its mouth.

Apogon maculatus
Small food items such as brine shrimps make ideal foods for this species.

SPHAERAMIA NEMATOPTERUS

PYJAMA CARDINALFISH

Unlike its cousin, *Apogon maculatus*, this species is from the Indo-Pacific. Indeed, it was first described from the Philippines, where it appears to be very common. The front part is a yellowish brown. Behind this is a dark-brownish vertical band joining the dorsal and pelvic fins, and then a pale, spotted area at the tail. As far as behavior and diet are concerned, it should be treated like *A. maculatus*.

Sphaeramia nematopterus
This species is displayed at its best as a group.

BALISTIDAE

TRIGGERFISHES

*T*he trigger-fishes are characterized by two unique physical attributes. The first spine of the dorsal fin is very large and, when erected, the small second spine locks it into place. This spine acts as a trigger – thus the name triggerfish – that must be released before the spine can be depressed. When danger threatens, triggerfishes take refuge in a crevice and raise this dorsal spine, effectively locking themselves in while still being able to snap at their attacker. The second characteristic is that their eyes are set at the top of a pretty long head, in effect keeping them away from the mouth and protecting them from the triggerfish's favorite food item, the sea urchin. The family members all have deep, laterally compressed bodies, no pelvic fins and separate, very sharp teeth, which come into their own when the animal is tackling its favorite food.

Triggerfishes are mostly found in shallow, tropical waters, although some

Balistidae

The eyes set at the top of a very high forehead give a clue to the triggerfish's natural diet of sea urchins.

do exist in the open ocean. Most species live either on coral reefs or in eelgrass beds. Some species are known to move into temperate seas during the warmer months. They reproduce in pits, which they dig in the sand within the female's territory. This territory will, in turn, be within the male's greater territory. Triggerfishes live alone in the wild and this is reflected in their behavior in captivity. In other words, the aquarist will find that to keep two triggerfishes – let alone two of the same species – is virtually impossible. Triggerfishes will eat almost anything, including prized invertebrates, so they should be kept in fish-only aquaria. They should also be kept well away from small fish species. Good choices of menu for them would be mussels, whole shrimps, and earthworms. Live river shrimps once or twice a week will also pay dividends as they help to keep the triggerfish's teeth worn down. Aquarium behavior will vary from the relatively benign to the downright aggressive. Some species will even rearrange the rockwork to their liking. However, triggerfish can quickly endear themselves to their owners to the extent that they take on full pet status.

Q I have an Undulate Triggerfish which keeps moving the rockwork around. Is this normal?

A Yes, very normal. This is one of the triggerfishes which likes to do that. You could try glueing the rock formations together so that they are too large for it to pick up.

BALISTAPUS UNDULATUS

UNDULATE TRIGGERFISH

*T*his species would be easier to keep if it were less aggressive and less prone to carrying items of decoration around in its mouth, which it will do with irritating regularity. *Balistapus undulatus* is found all over the vast Indo-Pacific region, with the exception of Hawaii. Its colors vary according to the area from which the specimen came. Fishes from the Indo-Pacific have orange tails, while specimens from the Pacific have green tails with orange rays. Males tend to be larger than females and lack any orange coloration around the head.

Balistapus undulatus

One of the most aggressive of all triggerfishes.

Balistes vetula

The filaments on this species' dorsal and anal fins grow with age.

BALISTES VETULA

QUEEN TRIGGERFISH

*L*ike *Balistapus undulatus*, this species would be easy to keep if it were not for its aggressive nature. *Balistes vetula* gains filaments on its dorsal and caudal fins as it grows, and these can become very long with age. Its home is the Western Atlantic, from New England, through the Caribbean to Brazil, where it is common on the reefs and around areas of seagrass down to depths of around 46 m (150 ft). Like the previous species, it will eat a wide variety of invertebrates and small fishes so must not be kept with them. Although this species can easily be hand-tamed, it should never be fed directly from the hand because of its natural aggression: always use tongs.

LENGTH IN WILD (IN)

LENGTH IN CAPTIVITY (IN)

HERBIVORE

OMNIVORE

PREDATOR

SINGLE SPECIMEN

COMMUNITY FISH

SAFE WITH SMALL FISHES

SAFE WITH INVERTEBRATES

EASE OF KEEPING FOR BEGINNERS (SCALE OF 1–10)

Balistes conspicullum

The hobbyist's favorite triggerfish.

BALISTOIDES CONSPICULLUM

CLOWN TRIGGER

*I*t is easy to see how this species got its popular name. Patterned with blotches, dashes and spots, it looks all dressed for fun. Unfortunately, fun isn't in this species' vocabulary. It can be a brute, although some specimens are very docile. Although this species is common around the reefs of the Indo-Pacific, it is relatively rare across its range, which extends as far as Australia and Japan. Its bright yellow mouth area helps to deter potential predators, while its pattern aids species recognition.

Q I have a 225 l (50 gal) aquarium which houses a King Angel and a lionfish. Could I add a triggerfish?

A Absolutely, as long as you do not overstock. Your tank probably only contains 180 l (40 gal) when displacement is accounted for, so your maximum fish-holding capacity is therefore 51 cm (20 in).

MELICHTHYS RINGENS

BLACK-FINNED TRIGGERFISH

*U*nlike the preceding species, this triggerfish is peaceful in captivity and can be trusted with small fishes, but not with invertebrates. Hailing from the Indo-Pacific, *M. ringens* is light brown overall, with black fins. It is set apart by the distinctive white lines at the base of the dorsal and anal fins. Like other triggerfish, it enjoys mussels, shrimps and live river shrimps. Notes given on keeping other triggerfish also apply to this species.

Melichthys ringens
Not all triggers are aggressive. This is one of the quietest of all triggerfishes.

Q Could I add a Queen Triggerfish to an aquarium which already holds a collection of small fishes and invertebrates?

A Absolutely not. The triggerfish would eat not only the invertebrates, but possibly the small fishes too.

ODONUS NIGER

BLACK (SOMETIMES BLUE) TRIGGERFISH

*T*his species' common name is something of a misnomer because its color can change from black to green, to blue, on a daily basis. It is found throughout the Indo-Pacific region and even the Red Sea. It is fairly common in shallow, inshore waters on the edge of coral reefs and over rough ground at depths of 9–30 m (30–100 ft). *Odonus niger* differs from other triggerfish species in that it has red teeth, is relatively peaceful in captivity and is a good choice for the beginner.

Odonus niger
The Black Triggerfish changes color on a daily basis.

Rhinecanthus aculeatus

One of the species within the family which likes to rearrange its living quarters.

RHINECANTHUS ACULEATUS

PICASSO TRIGGERFISH

*T*his species is even stranger to look at than *Balistoides conspicullum* and is even more easily identified. It could almost have been designed by Picasso as the patterns it displays look as though they were painted. This is another Indo-Pacific species, widely distributed from the East African coast, through the Indian Ocean and Western Pacific as far as Hawaii – where it is called *humuhumunukunkuapua'a*, which, roughly translated, means "the hog-snouted fish that fits things together." This is another species that likes to rearrange its home. This fish sleeps very soundly and emits a distinctive, whirring sound when startled.

BLENNIIDAE

BLENNIES

*T*his largish family of small, blunt-headed marine fishes is distributed worldwide. The blennies have scaleless skins and many small teeth. Some have large, curved, dagger-like paired teeth in the sides of their jaws. They have two long rays in each of their pelvic fins, and tufts of skin and tentacles over their eyes that help in distinguishing them from gobies. Blennies live in shallow, inshore waters, near to or on the bottom, where they rely on a secretive lifestyle and obliterative coloration for survival. Most blennies breed as they live, under rocks or in shells or crevices. The eggs are deposited in clumps and guarded by one or both of the adults. Blennies make super aquarium subjects, being extremely hardy and totally omnivorous. Even flake foods are taken enthusiastically. They make ideal additions to invertebrate aquariums as they generally leave everything else alone. One word of caution, however: some blennies are very territorial and should only be kept with fishes of at least twice their size.

Blenniidae

The Blennies have tentacles above their eyes – a characteristic which sets them apart from the Gobies.

Q I keep a 450 l (100 gal) reef aquarium which is a little devoid of movement. Amongst the species of fish I would like to add is the Bicolor Blenny. Would this be all right?

A Yes. *Escenius bicolor* is a wonderful choice for the invertebrate aquarium.

Aspidontus taeniatus
Avoid this species at all costs if you value your aquarium collection.

ASPIDONTUS TANIATUS

FALSE CLEANER FISH

This species is included only as a warning. On no account should it be introduced to a collection of coralfishes in captivity. This is because this species uses its close similarity to *Labroides dimidiatus* (the Cleaner Wrasse) to get close to its victims who, instead of the expected "wash and brush-up," are attacked. Study the differences between this species and *L. dimidiatus* carefully – the latter has an underslung mouth, for example – and avoid it at all costs.

This is a shy species which, nevertheless, is also very entertaining. It likes to live in small holes and caves, with only its head poking out. It darts out to catch its food and then darts back into its home, which it reenters by swimming past it a little way and then backing into the hole. This species is brown at the front and orange at the back. It is a wonderful aquarium choice, but be sure to provide a good choice of holes for it to live in.

Ecsenius bicolor
A wonderful choice for the invertebrate aquarium.

ECSENIUS BICOLOR

BICOLOR BLENNY

Ecsenius midas
Although this species may swim like an eel, it is a true Blenny.

KEY

LENGTH IN WILD (IN)

LENGTH IN CAPTIVITY (IN)

HERBIVORE

OMNIVORE

PREDATOR

SINGLE SPECIMEN

COMMUNITY FISH

SAFE WITH SMALL FISHES

SAFE WITH INVERTEBRATES

EASE OF KEEPING FOR BEGINNERS (SCALE OF 1–10)

ECSENIUS MIDAS
MIDAS BLENNY

 **8**

A native of the Indian Ocean and the Red Sea, this species swims very much like an eel, although it is hard to find two more unrelated species. It requires plenty of hiding places in the aquarium, but if you provide these you will find it very brave once it has settled in. Like the previous species, it will eat all the usual aquarium food and will live for years in either a fish-only or an invertebrate aquarium.

Also called the Striped Slimefish, this Indo-Pacific species has no cirri over the eyes, a feature that is indicative of blennies other than the genus *Petroscirtes*. The Scooter Blenny has a great following among invertebrate-aquarium fans, mainly because it can be kept in groups and is completely harmless to invertebrates. The males of this species have somewhat large dorsal fins, which they use to attract mates. All blenny requirements apply to this species, which is totally undemanding in captivity.

Petroscirtes temmincki
A very popular species – despite its alternative common name!

PETROSCIRTES TEMMINCKI
SCOOTER BLENNY

7

CALLIONYMIDAE

MANDARINS *and* DRAGONETS

*T*his family of small fishes, which live mostly in shallow waters, includes a few species that have become mainstays for hobbyists interested in keeping a complete coral reef in their homes. All have somewhat depressed body shapes, with broad pelvic fins just beneath the head. The gill openings are nothing more than round openings on either side of the head, in an almost dorsal position. This suits their natural lifestyle of lying on the bottom, sometimes completely buried in sand and fine gravel. The sexual differences within the group are, perhaps, the most notable feature of this family. Once they are sexually mature, the males are invariably brilliantly colored and have larger fins than the significantly drabber females and young fish. Some very elaborate courtship displays have been reported for some species, and sexual dimorphism – the occurrence of two distinct forms in the same species – is very common.

Although not much is known about the reproduction of this family, experts suggest that fertilization in some species is internal. The eggs are pelagic, which means that they are scattered in open water rather than being deposited on a surface (demersal). Very emaciated specimens are sometimes seen, and these should be avoided as they are doomed to die. Members of this family should never be kept with their own kind unless they are a matched pair. They can be aggressive, given their size, and will possibly fight to the death. The best type of aquarium for Mandarins and Dragonets are invertebrate aquariums – the type known as "miniature reefs" – because this type of aquarium will have a naturally occurring abundance of small animal life on which they can feed. They are particularly fond of copepods, small crustaceans that live in the sand of old, established tanks and when in competition with larger species, this is often the only food that they can get with any regularity.

Callionymidae

The Mandarins and Dragonets have become extremely popular with invertebrate-aquarium keepers.

Synchiropus picturatus
This species is a good choice for the invertebrate aquarium.

SYNCHIROPUS PICTURATUS
PSYCHEDELIC FISH

*This Pacific Ocean inhabitant comes mainly from the Philippines, but sometimes Melanesian specimens find their way into the trade. The *Synchiropus*

picturatus is becoming more common, especially in Europe, where it is possibly seen as a cheaper and more hardy alternative to *S. splendidus*. Both species are very long-lived in captivity provided that conditions are to their liking. They are, however, very shy and appreciate lots of hiding places.

Synchiropus splendidus
The pattern and coloration of this species is probably a danger warning.

SYNCHIROPUS SPLENDIDUS
MANDARINFISH

*Another Pacific species, S. splendidus looks very much like the previous species but has more red in its coloration. The green parts are also more green than in *S. picturatus* and this is the best way to distinguish between them. Like *S. picturatus*, this species likes a quiet aquarium, away from large boisterous species. Apparently, its mucus is poisonous and its gaudy coloration is possibly a warning of this. The same aquarium conditions as are needed for *S. picturatus* apply.

CHAETODONTIDAE

BUTTERFLYFISHES

*T*he butterfly-fishes are one of the most successful fish families in the world. There are some 120 species, around 90 percent of which live in the Indo-Pacific region. All members of the family are inhabitants of tropical and warm seas, and generally swarm over coral reefs, where their brilliant colors and patterns blend well with the surroundings. It is said that their multitudinous patterns help with species identification – particularly important for the continuation of the species.

Physically, they are brilliantly adapted to life in the wild. All members of the family possess compressed, deep bodies with particularly high backs, small mouths and tiny teeth. In fact, the word chaetodon, literally translated, means "bristle teeth." The small mouth and fine teeth are perfect for their favorite food – coral polyps, small worms and crustaceans. Color patterns vary tremendously within the family, and many species take on a nighttime coloration that is very different from their daytime one, presumably to avoid detection by predators while they are asleep. Butterflyfishes roam over fairly

Chaetodontidae
Butterflyfishes roam extensively during the day searching for food.

This is probably one reason why butterflyfishes have the reputation of being difficult to keep. This is particularly sad since, while many butterflyfishes are impossible to keep because they eat only coral polyps, there are many more that should pose no problems to an aquarist with a year's experience. The following species fall into the latter category, and the list at the end of this section shows those to avoid.

Whichever species you choose, you should observe a few basic rules. First, there should be no bullies or ebullient species in the aquarium – the best tank-mates for butterflyfishes are other butterflies. Although the aquarium should have plenty of swimming space, there should also be lots of nooks and crannies for the fish to retreat into at night. They should be offered a wide range of foods such as brine shrimps and bloodworms, or even large foods such as mussels broken into pieces that are small enough for the fishes' mouths. Despite what many authorities say, Chaetodons sometimes eat algae, so a substitute such as blanched lettuce should be offered if your aquarium does not have a natural growth of algae. Finally, it must be emphasized that the water quality must be absolutely perfect.

large areas during the day in their search for food. At night, however, most tend to retreat into a crevice or cave to sleep. They don't return to the same "bedroom" every night, but simply enter the nearest convenient one.

Their success in the wild is not, unfortunately, mirrored by their aquarium life. Many are bought by beginners with new aquariums or by aquarists who cannot feed them properly. Many more are housed in the wrong conditions or with the wrong type of fishes. Many hapless butterflies meet their ends at the hands of the inexperienced or unknowing hobbyist.

CHAETODON AURIGA

THREADFIN BUTTERFLYFISH

This species is one of the most popular and best known among aquarists and owes its popularity to its relatively undemanding nature and its longevity. Many scientists recognize two subspecies – *C. auriga auriga*, which is confined to the Red Sea, and *C. auriga setifa* from the Indo-Pacific. It is the latter that is usually seen in aquarium stores. *Chaetodon auriga* develops a false eye with maturity (unless it came from the Red Sea), and the first ray of its dorsal fin grows into the "thread" that gives the fish its common name. In keeping with many of its relatives, it also displays nighttime colors. Its daytime colors fade and a large, black undefined patch appears on its side. *Chaetodon auriga* will readily eat any of the usual aquarium food, but particularly relishes live brine shrimps.

Chaetodon auriga

If your threadfin has no false "eye," then it came from the Red Sea.

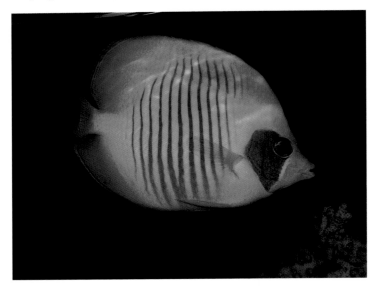

Coralfishes are kept for one of two reasons: either they are gorgeous to look at, or their behavior is interesting. Sometimes, as with this species, they are both. This distinctive fish, which is found only in the Red Sea, swarms over the coral reefs. It is relatively easy to keep, repaying the experienced aquarist with years of pleasure. It will eat almost any aquarium food and will live happily with its own kind. Unfortunately, like other Red Sea species, it is usually expensive. However, if you can afford the price, you will get a wonderful species in return.

Chaetodon semilarvatus

This species always comes from the Red Sea area and so is usually expensive.

CHAETODON SEMILARVATUS

GOLDEN BUTTERFLYFISH

CHAETODON VAGABUNDUS

VAGABOND BUTTERFLYFISH

6 4 7

Like *Hemitdurichthys zoster*, this species is hardy enough to be a beginner's fish, although it should never go into a totally new aquarium. This Indo-Pacific fish has a close cousin – *Chaetodon pictus* – that shares the same care requirements: no nitrites or ammonia in the water, no bullies and lots of live or freshly frozen, small food items such as brine shrimps and bloodworms.

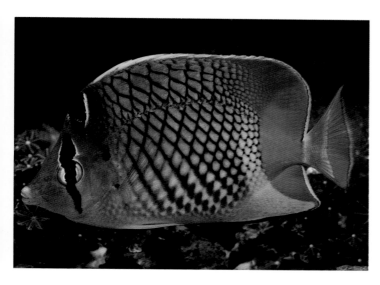

CHAETODON XANTHURUS

PEARLSCALE BUTTERFLYFISH

5 3-4 6

This species is found in the Indo-Pacific. One of a quartet of closely related and very similar species, all called pearlscales, it is the one most commonly encountered in captivity. *C. xanthurus* has been thought difficult to keep, and specimens from certain parts of the world can be fussy and pretty slow to settle in, sometimes dying before they have been acclimatized. However, it is one of the hardiest species in the family. It also has the advantage of being one of the few butterflyfish that lives happily with its own kind in captivity. Although no butterflyfish – with the possible exception of *Hemitaurichthys zoster* – can be described as suitable for beginners, this is a good choice for the aquarist new to butterflyfish.

FORCIPIGER FLAVISSIMUS

YELLOW LONG-NOSED

This striking species hails from the Indo-Pacific, as far as the Great Barrier Reef, and also the Red Sea. It is the most easily recognized of all the butterflyfish because of its long, slim snout. In fact, the snout is superbly modeled to allow the animal to poke it into crevices in search of food. It has a close cousin, *F. longirostris* (Big Yellow Long-nosed Butterflyfish), that has an even longer snout. That species, however, is seldom seen in captivity.

Despite the fragile-looking, tiny-mouthed long snout, *F. flavissimus* will eat most aquarium foods – even flake foods. It particularly relishes mussel meat but this has to be presented in the correct manner for the fish. It enjoys mussels whole but in the half-shell so that it can pick at it. Even more than other members of the family, *F. flavissimus* dislikes fast-swimming, ebullient species around it. A quiet aquarium – but not an invertebrate aquarium – suits it best. Water quality needs to be perfect, with no ammonia or nitrite present.

Forcipiger flavissimus

Although it may look somewhat fragile, this species is very hardy, provided that it is not kept with bullies.

Hemitaurichthys zosta

One of only two butterfly species which can be recommended to beginners.

HEMITAURICHTHYS ZOSTER

BLACK PYRAMID BUTTERFLYFISH

Of all the butterflyfishes kept by aquarists, this is one of only two that can truly be described as a beginner's fish. This Indo-Pacific species, which schools in massive swarms on the reef, is the strongest of all members of its family in captivity. It will eat anything at all, is peaceful and, unlike most of its cousins, will live with others of its own kind very happily in the aquarium. Like other members of the family, this species has nighttime colors. It becomes completely black, with just a spot remaining of its brilliant white, central flash. At first light, however, it changes back almost instantly. Its color also changes if it is annoyed, frightened or unhappy and so is also a good indicator of deteriorating water quality. If your *H. zoster* is showing no signs of being bullied or of fighting but has changed color in this way, then change some water.

HENIOCHUS ACUMINATUS

WIMPLE FISH

 8

Heniochus acuminatus is found all over the Indo-Pacific region and the Red Sea, ranging from there down the east coast of Africa, around the Cape and all over the Indian Ocean as far as Australia, the Philippines and Hawaii. It is, in fact, the most abundant of its genus. It lives exclusively on the coral reefs in its vast range, in shallow water down to depths of 30 m (100 ft). It is commonly seen living singly or in small groups in clear, shallow water. Unlike many of its cousins, this species positively welcomes other wimple fishes in the aquarium. Be warned, however, that the wimples that you buy at 5 cm (2 in) long can grow to be 15 cm (6 in) long. In a large enough aquarium, nevertheless, they are a tremendous sight.

An alternative common name for this species is Poor Man's Moorish Idol and, to some extent, it is strikingly similar to that species. However, the trained eye can easily distinguish between the two – whereas the Moorish Idol (*Zanclus canescens*) is vaguely triangular in shape, with almost no yellow in its coloration and a pronounced snout, the wimple is more rounded, with yellow dorsal and tail fins and forward-sloping back stripes. It is also very hardy, as opposed to the Moorish Idol, which is somewhat delicate. The first few dorsal rays are extended into a long streamer (the wimple), which increases in length with age. Specimens have been known to live to 13 years old in captivity, which is an indication of its aquarium suitability.

Heniochus acuminatus

"Poor Man's Moorish Idol" seems unfair; this species is fine in its own right.

KEY

LENGTH IN WILD (IN)

LENGTH IN CAPTIVITY (IN)

HERBIVORE

OMNIVORE

PREDATOR

SINGLE SPECIMEN

COMMUNITY FISH

SAFE WITH SMALL FISHES

SAFE WITH INVERTEBRATES

EASE OF KEEPING FOR BEGINNERS (SCALE OF 1–10) 7

CIRRHITIDAE

HAWKFISHES

The majority of this family of generally little, elongated fishes come from the Indo-Pacific, with just one of them being found in the tropical western Atlantic, around the Caribbean. They have two distinct dorsals – a spiny one, which gives way to a soft section. They also have three spines in front of the anal fin. Many of them have small tufts (cirri) on the membrane of the dorsal fin and a fringe at the rear of the front nostril. All members have elongated, separated lower rays to their pectoral fins, enabling them almost to sit on the seabed or on rocks and corals.

Hawkfishes live in shallow waters on the reef where they spend most of their time perched on some rock or coral head waiting for food – in the form of tiny, planktonic animals – to come along. When it does, the fish shoots from its perch to catch it, then returns just as quickly. Despite their cute looks, hawkfishes are predators which eat small fishes and crustaceans from the plankton. Two members of the family have become relatively important in the aquarium hobby, and they are shown here. They make good additions to the invertebrate or quiet, fish-only aquarium, although they should be kept well away from bullies. However, they will leave everything else alone (except some shrimps perhaps), including invertebrates. They should be fed small frozen foods and will be happy if given plenty of places where they can indulge in their naturally favorite pastime – perching.

Cirrhitidae

Hawkfishes spend much of their time perched among the coral, waiting for a tasty morsal to come past.

KEY

LENGTH IN WILD (IN)	
LENGTH IN CAPTIVITY (IN)	
HERBIVORE	
OMNIVORE	
PREDATOR	
SINGLE SPECIMEN	
COMMUNITY FISH	
SAFE WITH SMALL FISHES	
SAFE WITH INVERTEBRATES	
EASE OF KEEPING FOR BEGINNERS (SCALE OF 1–10)	

NEOCIRRHITES ARMATUS

SCARLET HAWKFISH

*T*his lovely little creature is not seen too often and so is usually expensive. However, dealers could sell twice as many as they can get at twice the price because it is a very popular species. It is not difficult to keep provided that its natural requirements are met – lots of perches and small foods – and will give its owner years of fishkeeping pleasure.

OXYCIRRHITES TYPUS

LONG-NOSED HAWKFISH

*E*ven hardier than the previous species, the female is somewhat larger than the male, which has a dark red lower jaw. This species is found in the East Indies and around Mauritius and is unmistakable because of its relatively enormous, pointed snout. That snout is perfect for probing into crevices for food items. Some aquarium spawnings have been reported, the eggs being laid on a flat site in patches. This species' "check" pattern helps to camouflage it as it perches among the coral. Like *Neocirrhites armatus*, it does tremendously well in an invertebrate aquarium.

DIODONTIDAE

PORCUPINEFISHES

You will often hear people speaking of porcupinefishes and calling them pufferfishes. Yet, despite the similarities between the two families – pufferfishes are discussed elsewhere – they are separate defined families. There are two porcupine species of importance to the hobbyist, and both are shown here. The porcupinefishes have teeth that are fused together in each jaw to form a sharp beak. Their bodies are covered in long, thick spines which lie flat when the animal is just going about its daily business. When it is threatened by a predator, it inflates itself with water and the spines stick out, turning it into a formidable mouthful. As well as this ability to inflate itself, the porcupinefish has another trick: some species have marks on the back that, when the fish is inflated, look like big, glaring "eyes."

Porcupinefishes are found all over the world in tropical climates, yet very few species are known. In fact, some experts believe there are only 15. In some parts of the world their flesh is considered poisonous and in others it is not: in Japan the chefs are well-trained in their preparation. Porcupinefishes are probably best known to dwellers of temperate lands as lampshades – their skin having been inflated and dried out. They are then hung in bars and shops. On the coral reefs, however, they are often very abundant and are important members of the fauna.

Porcupinefishes quickly take on full pet status. They should be fed large food items, preferably mussels, lancefishes and – most important – crustaceans with their exoskeletons still intact. This last item, when fed regularly, will help to regulate their teeth. They obviously need plenty of swimming space, so they should not be considered for aquariums of less than 375 l (80 gal) capacity. They should also be kept well away from small fishes and all invertebrates.

Diodontidae
Porcupinefishes quickly assume pet status.

Diodon holocanthus

A voracious predator, but a real pet.

DIODON HOLOCANTHUS
LONG-SPINED PORCUPINEFISH

This species is the most common in aquarium stores. It is the most appealing species in the hobby, but it is also a voracious predator that will eat any species that it can get into its mouth. Having said that, it is very gratifying to keep as it is extremely hardy and long-lived.

DIODON HYSTRIX
COMMON PORCUPINEFISH

Unlike *D. holocanthus*, this species is not active during the day, but prefers to hide in caves for long periods until its hunger gets the better of it. Everything regarding the care of *D. holocanthus* also applies to this species.

Diodon hystrix

An aquarium of at least 375 l (80 gal) and good filtration are essential.

GOBIIDAE

GOBIES

*T*he gobies are one of the most successful fish families in temperate and tropical waters. Being extremely abundant in coastal and inshore waters it also enters freshwater, and several purely freshwater species have evolved as a result. The gobies possess pelvic fins that have fused together to form a cup, a characteristic they do not share with the blennies, the family they are commonly confused with. This fusion helps them to stay orientated in the intertidal waters that are their main habitat. Gobies are rather small, thick-set fishes. They have two dorsal fins, the first of which has weak spines.

The majority of gobies live in crevices or close to the seabed, where they exist by grubbing out small animal life or, sometimes, planktonic animals. Although some members of the family can reach 30 cm (12 in) when fully adult, the more usual size is around 2.5–5 cm (1–2 in). In fact, the smallest fishes in the world (*Eviota mistyctbis* and *Pandaka*) are gobies.

Gobies all do well in the aquarium as long as the conditions are right – a quiet, preferably invertebrate, aquarium with plenty of nooks and crannies. They should be fed on small frozen foods such as brine shrimps, bloodworms, fish eggs and mussels, or similar, finely chopped. Gobies will spawn readily in captivity. They also act as cleaners of other species in much the same way as *Labroides dimidiatus*.

Gobiidae
Gobies will spawn readily in captivity.

GOBIODON CITRINUS
LEMON GOBY

 6

Gobiodon citrinus
Although this species will eat any aquarium food, it particularly relishes brine shrimps.

This small Indo-Pacific species has a poisonous mucus coating that protects it from predators. It is a very striking species, being solid yellow with electric blue flashes around its eyes, gills, and immediately below its dorsal fins. Once it is acclimatized, it will eat almost anything of the correct size, and particularly relishes brine shrimps.

Q I have just bought a lovely little fish called a Lemon Goby. What do I feed it on?

A One of the golden rules of fish-keeping is to do some homework on a species before you buy it. You have broken this rule but, fortunately, have got away with it. The Lemon Goby will eat most aquarium foods, but will relish live brine shrimps.

GOBIODON OKINAWAE

YELLOW GOBY

 6

Gobiodon okinawae
Even though the Yellow Goby is peaceful with other species, it will fight with its own kind.

*T*he gobies would be much easier to keep if they weren't so small. As it is, depending on their tank-mates, their diminutive size can cause problems. However, in a quiet invertebrate aquarium all should be all right. This species has a tendency to fight with its own kind, so keep only one at a time. It is extremely peaceful with anything else, however, so can be kept with most other species provided that they are not predators. This species is found in the Pacific Ocean.

Gobiosoma oceanops
A wonderful breeding prospect.

GOBIOSOMA OCEANOPS

NEON GOBY

 7

*G*obiosoma oceanops comes from the Western Atlantic and is probably the most familiar goby among marine aquarists, mainly because of its dazzling colors and the fact that most successful breeding reports involving gobies are of this species. The beginner will find this a wonderful fish to keep in a group of five or six as long as there are no predators present. It also offers a cleaning service for other fishes. Being so tiny, its lifespan is relatively short, about two years being the norm. However, because it spawns so regularly, you will have the opportunity to raise a few generations as long as the conditions are right. It feeds on parasites, plankton and small crustaceans.

Lythrypnus dalli
Not a true tropical animal, although it will thrive in a tropical invertebrate aquarium.

KEY

LENGTH IN WILD (IN)	
LENGTH IN CAPTIVITY (IN)	
HERBIVORE	
OMNIVORE	
PREDATOR	
SINGLE SPECIMEN	
COMMUNITY FISH	
SAFE WITH SMALL FISHES	
SAFE WITH INVERTEBRATES	
EASE OF KEEPING FOR BEGINNERS (SCALE OF 1–10)	7

LYTHRYPNUS DALLI
CATALINA GOBY

*T*his species does equally well in a tropical or temperate environment. Found along the Californian coast, it inhabits shallow, inshore waters and feeds – as most of its family do – on small crustaceans and other tiny organisms. It will live happily with others of its own kind, but make sure that no predators are present. Another short-lived species, *L. dalli* is best exhibited in an invertebrate aquarium where it will show its natural behavior to the full.

Valenciennea strigata
This constantly sifts the substrate for food, keeping the filter bed free of blockages.

VALENCIENNEA STRIGATA
BLUE-CHEEK GOBY

*I*n the wild this species, from the Western Pacific and Indian Ocean, spends much of its day digging and sifting the sand looking for food items. It will carry over this natural behavior into the aquarium. This goby will happily tolerate others of the same species in the aquarium, and can be kept in pairs with no problems. Easy to keep, although best displayed in an invertebrate collection, this species can be kept in a fish-only aquarium without looking out of place.

GRAMMIDAE

FAIRY BASSLETS

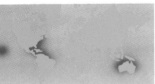

*T*he fairy basslets are a small family of beautiful, tropical marine fishes found mainly in the Western Atlantic and around the Caribbean, although some species come from Hawaii and tropical Australia. However, some authorities believe they are all from the Caribbean, hence defining them from the dottybacks described later. The fairy basslets are closely related to the Serranidae family, the sea basses, but differ from them in having an uninterrupted lateral line – or none at all – and a single, continuous dorsal fin with 11–13 spines and soft rays. The pelvic fins have five rays and one spine. Being another family that spends most of its time hiding in the many crevices and caves found in a coral reef, they are shy and very territorial in nature. They live somewhat solitary lives, coming together only for spawning. In view of this natural behavior, they should be kept alone unless you have a sufficiently large aquarium to keep them well apart.

There are just three known species in the Grammidae family, two of which are seen in the hobby. The third – *Gramma linki* – is so rare that it is seldom seen, even in the wild. These fish eat mainly planktonic animals in the wild and, although they will eat flake food when they are acclimatized, they have to be fed on live or frozen brine shrimps as their staple diet.

Grammidae
Closely related to the family Serranidae, this family contains only three species.

Gramma loreto
One of the most spectacularly colored species in the hobby.

LENGTH IN WILD (IN)

LENGTH IN CAPTIVITY (IN)

HERBIVORE

OMNIVORE

PREDATOR

SINGLE SPECIMEN

COMMUNITY FISH

SAFE WITH SMALL FISHES

SAFE WITH INVERTEBRATES

EASE OF KEEPING FOR BEGINNERS (SCALE OF 1–10) | 7 |

GRAMMA LORETO
ROYAL GRAMMA

This small species from the Western Atlantic spends much of its time lying in caves and beneath overhangs, orienting itself so that it is pressed against the substrate and often lying upside down as a result. The spectacular coloration of this species – violet at the front and yellow at the back, two golden streaks on the head and a black spot on the dorsal fin – has made this species a great favorite with marine fishkeepers. However, it is a highly territorial species that resents the presence of others with the same disposition. It should be fed on small food items such as chopped shrimp and brine shrimps. It should, of course, be provided with plenty of caves and hiding places. An ideal addition to the invertebrate aquarium, it can also thrive in a quiet, fish-only collection.

Gramma malecara
This species can be so aggressive that it will literally bite the hand that feeds it.

GRAMMA MALECARA
BLACK-CAPPED GRAMMA

This Caribbean species is very striking, with its distinctive, purple body and black "cap." Even more territorial than *G. loreto*, this species can become so aggressive that it will bite the hand that feeds it. However, its appearance makes it a superb addition to any invertebrate aquarium.

HAEMULIDAE

GRUNTS

Members of this family are very similar to the snappers, differing only in their dentition. They are given the popular name of grunts because of the way that many grind their pharyngeal teeth, the sound being amplified by the swimbladder. By and large, this family is unknown in the aquarium hobby – only the porkfish is kept by hobbyists – because grunts are too large for the average aquarium. This is a pity because they can make striking additions to a good-sized fish-only aquarium containing large, mainly predatory and aggressive species. They should be housed in at least 375 l (100 gal) tank with heavy, efficient filtration and good water flow. They are messy eaters with huge appetites, and love to tear apart large food items, including small fishes, mussels and other meaty foods. Without efficient filtration, the water quality will deteriorate rapidly, with dire consequences. Unfortunately, grunts quickly outgrow all but the largest aquarium.

Haemulidae

The grunts get their popular name from the way in which they grind their pharyngeal teeth.

KEY

LENGTH IN WILD (IN)

LENGTH IN CAPTIVITY (IN)

HERBIVORE

OMNIVORE

PREDATOR

SINGLE SPECIMEN

COMMUNITY FISH

SAFE WITH SMALL FISHES

SAFE WITH INVERTEBRATES

EASE OF KEEPING FOR BEGINNERS (SCALE OF 1–10) 7

ANISOTREMUS VIRGINICUS

PORKFISH

*T*his Caribbean species will live happily with its own kind in a large aquarium. As juveniles, they are very striking, with silvery cream bodies, yellow heads, black stripes and a black patch on the caudal peduncle. The adults, however, become very drab in comparison. First-class filtration is mandatory with this species.

Anisotremus virginicus
A large aquarium with efficient filtration is mandatory for this species.

Q I have a really large aquarium (675 l/150 gal) which is now mature. I like large fishes, but would also like a shoal of one single species. Which one do you suggest?

A There are one or two species you could consider. My favorite choice would be a group of porkfishes. They make messes, however, so be sure that your filtration is up to standard.

HOLOCENTRIDAE

SQUIRRELFISHES

Sometimes called soldierfishes, this family is widely distributed in warm and tropical seas, where members inhabit rocky areas or coral reefs. In spite of this wide distribution, there are relatively few members of the family. Most are brightly colored, with red predominating. This is entirely due to their nocturnal lifestyle, as are their large eyes. They have heavy, rough scales, dorsal and anal spines, and spiny heads. One genus – *Holocentrus*, to which all the species discussed here belong – has a heavy spine at the corner of each gill cover. Most squirrelfishes lead an entirely nocturnal existence, spending the daylight hours in a cave or crevice, coming out only at night to feed. They are noisy fishes, having the ability to click or creak loudly underwater. As a family they are very active and will need to be housed in a large aquarium. This energetic lifestyle may not suit quieter species. Despite their nocturnal existence in the wild, squirrelfishes will eventually adapt to aquarium life and swim around in daylight hours with the other occupants. Until they do adapt, however, give newly imported specimens plenty of hiding places. They like to eat chopped earthworms, small fishes, and mussels.

Holocentridae

The Squirrelfishes are all large, nocturnal predators.

KEY

LENGTH IN WILD (IN)

LENGTH IN CAPTIVITY (IN)

HERBIVORE

OMNIVORE

PREDATOR

SINGLE SPECIMEN

COMMUNITY FISH

SAFE WITH SMALL FISHES

SAFE WITH INVERTEBRATES

EASE OF KEEPING FOR BEGINNERS (SCALE OF 1–10)

HOLOCENTRUS DIADEMA

COMMON SQUIRRELFISH

Holocentrus diadema
Easy to adapt to an aquarium lighting regime.

A large species that is often seen in its native Indo-Pacific, this hardy fish provides a striking addition to a fish-only tank. Do not, however, try to keep it with small fishes – the latter will quickly become an expensive meal.

KEY

 LENGTH IN WILD (IN)

 LENGTH IN CAPTIVITY (IN)

 HERBIVORE

 OMNIVORE

 PREDATOR

 SINGLE SPECIMEN

 COMMUNITY FISH

 SAFE WITH SMALL FISHES

 SAFE WITH INVERTEBRATES

 EASE OF KEEPING FOR BEGINNERS (SCALE OF 1–10)

Holocentrus rufus
One glance at the white triangular markings will tell you how this species gets its common name.

HOLOCENTRUS RUFUS

WHITE-TIPPED SQUIRRELFISH

This Western Atlantic species can be kept with some invertebrates, but not with small crustaceans. It looks similar to all squirrelfishes, but has a white, triangular mark on each of its dorsal spines. It is a bold animal which will respond to any threats with an audible grunting.

MYRIPRISTIS MURDJAN

BIG-EYED SQUIRRELFISH

This relatively peaceful species hails from the Indo-Pacific and lacks the spine on the gill cover that members of the genus *Holocentrus* have. This species may prove more difficult to adapt to a normal daylight existence in the aquarium and, though peaceful, will eat any small fishes which share its quarters.

Myripristis murdian
Although peaceful, this species should not be kept with small fishes.

*L*ABRIDAE

WRASSES

Labridae

There are about 400 species of Wrasse, some of which have become firm aquarium favorites.

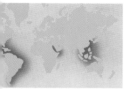

*T*his large, successful family of some 400 species has become one of the mainstays of the aquarium hobby over the years, with members from all seas and of all shapes and sizes, and displaying all types of behavior. Members are characterized by a single dorsal fin, the spiny part of which is considerably larger than the soft-rayed part. Most have thick lips, well-developed teeth in the jaws and large crushing teeth in the pharynx. As a group, the wrasses are colorful, and there are usually considerable differences between the adult males and the females, and juveniles. As a result of this, some species have been named more than once, so that the 400 members mentioned earlier could be inflated. Sex changes from female to male are common.

Many species of wrasse (notably *Labroides dimidiatus*) have been found to clean parasites from other species, and interesting breeding behavior is commonplace. Elaborate pre-spawning displays are performed, and some species build nests out of plant material that are guarded by the male. The family is well known for sleeping at night either completely buried in the sand or wedged between rocks. Some scientists even suggest that wrasses dream.

BODIANUS PULCHELLUS

CUBAN HOGFISH

A Western Atlantic species that ranges from South Carolina to Florida and the Bahamas and as far south as the Ascension Islands, this deep-water fish is found on steep-sloping reef faces at depths of 24 m (78 ft). It is highly prized among aquarists and is usually easy to acclimatize to aquarium life because of its catholic tastes in food. It should not be kept in an invertebrate aquarium because, although it is safe when very young, when grown it will make a meal of any crustaceans and probably most other inhabitants too. Small fishes are also in danger, so it is best kept with species that are larger than the wrasse. It should be fed as varied a diet as possible, which it will take eagerly.

Bodianus pulchellus
Simple to keep, but a danger to invertebrates and small fishes.

BODIANUS RUFUS

SPANISH HOGFISH

L ooking very similar to B. *pulchellus*, this fish lives on reefs from Bermuda in the north, down through the Caribbean to South America. It has a similar lifestyle to B. *pulchellus* with the exception that it lives in much shallower waters. In the wild the juveniles are known to be cleaners of parasites from other species, while the adults live on crabs, sea urchins and mollusks. Aquarium requirements and care are the same as for B. *pulchellus*.

Bodianus rufus
As with its cousin, B. *pulchellus*, keep this beast well away from invertebrates in the aquarium.

Coris angulata
Called the Napoleon Wrasse when fully grown, this species will eventually outgrow even the largest home aquarium.

CORIS ANGULATA

TWIN-SPOT WRASSE

This species comes from the Red Sea and the Indo-Pacific, where it lives in the shallow waters of the reef. This astonishing fish will grow from an attractive juvenile into a massive, hump-headed monster 1.2 m (4 ft) long if it has the chance. This will never happen in the aquarium, however, although *C. angulata* will grow very quickly and change color dramatically. The spots will disappear, it will turn to green with yellow-edged fins, and it will be called the Napoleon Wrasse.

While it is a juvenile *C. angulata* is a lovely aquarium subject although, like other members of the family, it should never be trusted with invertebrates.

Coris formosa
Take care with small fishes when this species is fully grown.

CORIS FORMOSA

AFRICAN CLOWN WRASSE

This species – widely distributed throughout the Indo-Pacific – buries itself in the sand to sleep and also when danger threatens. This behavior, along with its vibrant juvenile coloration and strange swimming style make it one of the favorites among wrasses. While the adult is comparatively drab, it is still attractive, being brown-green with two blue-green stripes that run from in front of and behind the gill cover. This species is safe with smaller fishes when it is young, but care must be taken with adults. The same applies with invertebrates. This species enjoys live brine shrimps and other small meaty foods.

CORIS GAIMARDI
CLOWN WRASSE

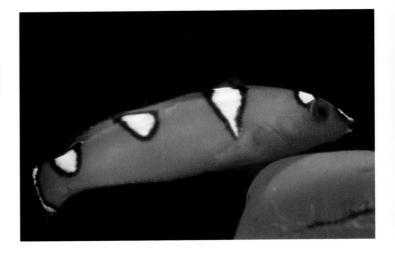

This species is very similar to *C. formosa*, except that it is red rather than brown and the white bands on its head and around the dorsal area don't extend so far down the body. It buries itself to sleep and whenever danger looms. It also tends to be very nervous, so make sure it is not shocked. All of the points made regarding aquarium care of *C. formosa* apply to this species.

Coris gaimardi
Like the previous species, this is one of the burrowing wrasses, so a good depth of substrate is required for it to be happy when in captivity.

Labroides dimidiatus
This species is invaluable for keeping parasites at bay in the aquarium.

LABROIDES DIMIDIATUS
CLEANER WRASSE

This wonderful fish comes from the Indo-Pacific and the Red Sea through to the central Pacific Ocean. It is readily available and should be on everyone's stocking list. *Labroides dimidiatus* is the biggest ally against the onslaught of parasites that the marine aquarist could have. When fully acclimatized it will spend its day soliciting clients for its services, and then proceed all over its tankmate's body and into its gills and mouth, ridding it of parasites just as it would in the wild. If you keep two specimens, they will replicate their natural behavior by setting up a cleaning station — something that lone cleaners tend not to do in captivity. This behavior is not altogether altruistic because, as the fish performs this very necessary (and engaging) service, it also gets its natural diet. In this way, *L. dimidiatus* will keep parasites and pathogens in check, preventing a catastrophic outbreak. Small, meaty foods should supplement the cleaner's natural diet admirably.

LIENARDELLA FASCIATUS

HARLEQUIN TUSKFISH

This Pacific Ocean species looks, to the casual observer, very aggressive. In fact this striking species is a mild-mannered, community animal that can be mixed with most species provided that they are too large to fit in its mouth. However, on no account should it be kept with invertebrates. With orange stripes on a silver background, it graces any fish-only aquarium and is easy to keep. Fed on a varied diet of meaty type foods, it will stay happy in your aquarium for years.

Lienardella fasciatus

Although this species may look ferocious, it is fine with all but the smallest of fishes.

The most notable characteristic of this Indo-Pacific species is its seemingly inexhaustible energy. It will swim all day, in an almost unique, dolphin-like manner, covering every inch of the aquarium until nighttime, when it sleeps in a shell or crevice. At first light it is up and about again for another busy day. Although this fish will live happily in a community of similarly sized species, it will attack smaller species, and two kept together will fight unmercifully. With that caveat in mind, however, *T. lunare* is a terrific aquarium species that will live for years in a well filtered tank. It feeds on the usual aquarium foods, including invertebrates, so keep it in a fish-only aquarium.

Thalassoma lunare

A tireless swimmer, this species should never be trusted in a tank with invertebrates.

THALASSOMA LUNARE

LYRETAIL WRASSE

LUTJANIDAE

SNAPPERS

*T*he snapper family is represented throughout the world. They are generally large, with high foreheads, large canine-like teeth situated in the jaws and an upper jaw that moves freely in an upward direction. All family members are scaled over the body and most of the head, and the dorsal fin is continuous. The family is very abundant in tropical waters and some of them are important as food fish, although in some parts of the world they are known to cause ciguatera, a serious form of fish poisoning. This is passed through the food chain from one fish to another, starting with those that feed on poisonous algae.

There are some 300 species in the family, very few of which are of any importance to the aquarium hobbyist. The main two species are discussed here. Both have the capacity to grow very large, even in the aquarium, and should be kept with other large, strong species in an aquarium that is heavily filtered and aerated. They should be kept well away from small fishes and invertebrates and provided with a varied diet of lancefishes, mussels, shrimps and so on. They will also eat earthworms.

Lutjanidae

Although this family consists of 300 members, only two or three are of any interest to the hobby.

Lutjanus sebae
This species is a highly prized sport fish all over the world.

LUTJANUS SEBAE
EMPEROR SNAPPER

This beauty is found in the Indo-Pacific, from the East African coast, throughout the Indian Ocean, through to Australia and the Western Pacific, on coral reefs and in sandy and rocky areas. It is an important food fish everywhere, as well as being a highly prized game fish. Particularly handsome when young (up to about 30 cm/12 in long) with vivid red bands on its middle and two inwardly pointing bars on the head and tail, *L. sebae* turns relatively dull as it matures, with the red turning to pink. It is only of interest to the aquarist as a juvenile and even then needs plenty of room. Make sure that there are no small fishes in its tank or it will soon make a meal of them – and definitely no invertebrates for the same reason.

Symphorichthys spilurus
Keep this species well away from potential fin-nippers.

SYMPHORICHTHYS SPILURUS
MAJESTIC SNAPPER

This Pacific Ocean species is nowhere near as large as *Lutjanus sebae* and so can be considered a community species, but two will fight so only a single specimen should be kept. It needs plenty of space, and no potential fin-nippers should be housed with it or the long filaments on its dorsal and anal fins won't be long for very long. Feed large, meaty foods such as lancefishes and mussels. No small fishes or invertebrates should be in the aquarium.

MICRODESMIDAE

FIREFISHES

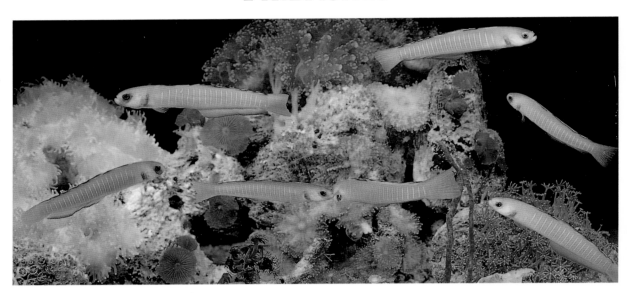

*U*nlike the last family, this group make excellent additions to the invertebrate aquarium. This is a family of small fishes from the coral reefs of the Indian, Pacific and Western Atlantic oceans and also the Caribbean region. Most of the family are extremely elongated and slender, and are sometimes known as wormfishes. Most are scaleless or have minute, embedded scales. The lower jaw projects and the dorsal and anal fins have long bases and are attached to the tail. The small size of these fishes has meant that classifying them has always been difficult, some members having been grouped with the blennies in the past. Others have been grouped with the eleotids and others again with the gobies. It is now recognized that, though they are closely related to the blennies, they are a family in their own right. Firefishes hover just over the reef, against the current, feeding on plankton. However, whenever danger looms, they quickly dart into their own crevice in the reef.

In all species, the first ray of the dorsal spine is greatly extended, and probably acts as a signal to others in the group. It is also possible that these fishes use their spines to lock themselves into crevices as a defence against predators.

In the aquarium these fishes may prove somewhat nervous, so they need lots of hideouts to retreat into when they feel threatened. A group of firefishes may be kept together, but each will need a good amount of space. They will establish a hierarchy, with the most dominant taking the best position.

Microdesmidae
Closely related to the blennies, this family does superbly in the invertebrate aquarium.

**Nemateleotris
decora**

A popular species with
invertebrate-aquarium
keepers.

NEMATELEOTRIS DECORA

PURPLE FIREFISH

3 1½-2 6

This small, beautiful fish from the Indo-Pacific does well in a quiet invertebrate aquarium, but not so in a tank of boisterous species. It is relatively rare and very attractive and, as a result, is usually comparatively expensive. Feed them on small frozen foods, such as brine shrimps.

**Nemateleotris
magnifica**

Being of a nervous
disposition, this species
can be very difficult to
keep.

NEMATELEOTRIS MAGNIFICA

FIREFISH

2½ 1 6

This species has a nervous disposition and is therefore not easy to keep. However, if the correct environment is provided, there should not be a problem. It has a much longer dorsal ray than *N. decora* and is further distinguished by its lighter, more creamy-pink color. Keep as for *N. decora*.

MONOCANTHIDAE

FILEFISHES

The filefishes are very closely related to the triggerfishes and, like that group have two dorsal fins, the first of which has a spine that can be locked into position. The ventral fins are merely a single spine and their mouths are tiny. The skin is very rough to the touch and this has led to them being given the alternative name of leatherjackets. Curiously, most of the species in the family are found only around Australia, where they make use of their unusual appearance to hide among floating seaweed.

In spite of their physiological similarity to the triggerfishes, filefishes are very quiet in the aquarium, although they can take a while to acclimatize to a captive way of life because they can be difficult to wean onto alternatives to their natural diet of coral polyps and algae. However, once they have adapted, they will happily live on all normal aquarium foods. Live foods will start the weaning process, and should gradually be replaced with frozen foods until the fish is eating nothing but frozen foods, although live foods should be given as an occasional treat. Filefishes will do best in a quiet aquarium containing species such as butterflyfishes.

Monocanthidae
This family is very closely related to the triggerfishes.

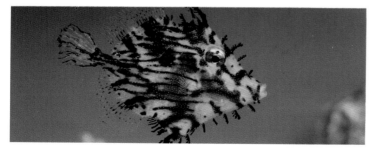

Chaetodermis pencilligerus
Do not keep this with invertebrates, as its natural diet includes coral polyps.

CHAETODERMIS PENCILLIGERUS

TASSELLED FILEFISH

This Indo-Pacific species makes a striking and unusual specimen in any aquarium, provided that all the other inmates are of a similar disposition, which means no bullies or ebullient, fast-swimming species. This fish's natural diet consists of coral polyps, so it cannot be kept with invertebrates.

MONOCENTRIDAE

PINECONE FISHES

KEY

LENGTH IN
WILD (IN)

LENGTH IN
CAPTIVITY (IN)

HERBIVORE

OMNIVORE

PREDATOR

SINGLE SPECIMEN

COMMUNITY FISH

SAFE WITH
SMALL FISHES

SAFE WITH
INVERTEBRATES

EASE OF KEEPING
FOR BEGINNERS
(SCALE OF 1–10) 7

Only two species of this remarkable family are known and they are both found in the Indo-Pacific. Both are plump and rounded, with heads covered in bone and bodies encased by heavy scales to form a formidable body armor. The dorsal spines are large and sharp, lying alternately from left to right, while the pelvic spines are massive. A pinecone fish would be a nasty mouthful for any predator.

These fishes come from deep water and so are only occasionally seen in the aquarium trade. As a result of this, and their novelty value, they command a high price, but it is well worth paying the necessary price as they make the most interesting of aquarium subjects. They are best kept in a species tank.

Monocentris japonicus
Low light levels will show these animals at their best.

MONOCENTRIS JAPONICUS

PINECONE FISH

This species is widely distributed in the Indo-Pacific from South Africa through to Japan, where it is eaten. These animals come from deep water so a species tank with low light levels will make them feel at home. They have symbiotic bacteria within their heads that light up – it is thought to attract prey – which looks terrific. Their natural diet is open to debate, but in captivity they seem to do well on meaty frozen food and chopped, white fish.

MURAENIDAE

MORAY EELS

The moray eels have historically been seen in a similar light to sharks – vicious predators that also like to harm humans. As is the case with sharks, moray eels are for the most part much maligned and misunderstood. They are also harmless to humans if handled correctly. Morays have become notorious because of their habit of lying in a cave with their heads sticking out and their jaws gaping open, displaying fearsome-looking teeth. They do this, however, in order to get water over their gills so that they can breathe.

There can be danger attached to keeping moray eels, and the rule is never to hand-feed one. They have very poor eyesight and hunt by smell, attacking the scent of their meal rather than the sight of it. They also have very sharp, filthy teeth. If you wave a piece of fish in front of a moray, it will lunge at a vague area of smell and could well get your hand instead of the food, giving you a nasty wound that will, by virtue of those teeth, probably become infected. Another danger is that they could eat everything else in the aquarium, so make sure that there are no small or slow-swimming species housed with a moray. Despite all this, moray eels – in the right type of collection – can be amazing.

Moray eels are the most abundant and widely distributed family of eels, found all over the world in tropical and temperate waters. Many are brightly patterned and a few are very long, up to 3 m (10 ft) having been recorded. However, the species of interest to the aquarist rarely grow larger than 61 cm (24 in) in captivity. They should be fed on large meaty items.

Muraenidae

Much maligned and misunderstood, the Moray Eels are, to all intents and purposes, totally harmless – provided you do not hand-feed them.

Q What is the best type of fish to keep with a Moray Eel?

A Species like porcupine pufferfishes, triggerfishes, lionfishes and large angelfishes are the best to keep with moray eels. There are others, of course, so do some reading before choosing.

KEY

LENGTH IN WILD (IN)	
LENGTH IN CAPTIVITY (IN)	
HERBIVORE	
OMNIVORE	
PREDATOR	
SINGLE SPECIMEN	
COMMUNITY FISH	
SAFE WITH SMALL FISHES	
SAFE WITH INVERTEBRATES	
EASE OF KEEPING FOR BEGINNERS (SCALE OF 1–10)	

Echnida nebulosa
Probably the most commonly seen Moray species in the hobby.

ECHNIDA NEBULOSA
SNOWFLAKE MORAY

This species is probably the most popular with aquarists, no doubt because it stays a manageable size. Its distinctive black and white pattern explains its popular name. It comes from the Indo-Pacific and, like all morays, should not be kept with invertebrates or small fishes, and should never be hand-fed. This species is particularly fond of live river shrimp in the aquarium.

KEY

 LENGTH IN WILD (IN)

 LENGTH IN CAPTIVITY (IN)

 HERBIVORE

 OMNIVORE

 PREDATOR

 SINGLE SPECIMEN

 COMMUNITY FISH

 SAFE WITH SMALL FISHES

 SAFE WITH INVERTEBRATES

 7 EASE OF KEEPING FOR BEGINNERS (SCALE OF 1–10)

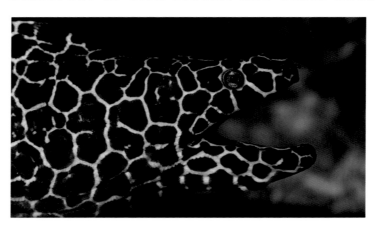

Gymnothorax tesselatus

Only aquarists with large aquariums should consider keeping this beast.

GYMNOTHORAX TESSELATUS

LEOPARD MORAY

*B*eing much larger, both in length and girth, than *Echnida nebulosa*, this species – also from the Indo-Pacific – is for large tanks only. It is very predatory and will eat anything it can swallow, so large tankmates are necessary. Apart from this it would be relatively easy to keep, being easily pleased with regard to food and water quality.

Rhinomuraenia ambionensis

Not really a species for the beginner.

RHINOMURAENIA AMBIONENSIS

BLUE-RIBBON EEL

*T*his Pacific Ocean species is definitely not easy to keep. It is somewhat sensitive and more than a little cranky. It seems that specimens either do well in captivity or die. Therefore, it is not recommended for the beginner. A skilled aquarist may be able to achieve success with it, provided that they can provide top-quality conditions.

OPISTOGNATHIDAE

JAWFISHES

This is a small family of shallow-water fishes found in the Western Atlantic and the Indian and Pacific Oceans. Their popular name, jawfish, comes from their very pronounced jaws. Most species are somewhat slender, with well-developed, long-based dorsal and anal fins. Some forms live in vertical burrows, which they line with shells and into which they retreat tail first. They will carry this activity over into the aquarium and even use a small stone or shell to cover the entrance at night. Some species undergo color changes at breeding time, when the males tend to incubate the eggs in their mouths.

They can be housed as a group,

but must be provided with plenty of hiding places. They will always stay close to, or inside their burrows, awaiting their next meal. In the wild, this takes the form of small fishes and crustaceans that pass by in the current. They take off like jet planes to grab a morsel of food from above, and can also jump out of their tank very easily.

Opistognathidae
Species in this group need lots of hiding places if they are to be happy in captivity.

OPISTOGNATHUS AURIFRONS

YELLOW-HEADED JAWFISH

With a delicate yellow head and gorgeous pale blue body, this species will adorn any invertebrate aquarium. With equally peaceful tank-mates it can also be kept in a fish-only collection, provided that all its other physical needs are met. This Western Atlantic species needs a softish, deep substrate, such as coral sand, into which it can dig its burrows. Feed it on small food items such as brine shrimps.

Opistognathus aurifrons
Feed this on small items, provide plenty of substrate and this species will live a long and happy life.

OSTRACION

BOXFISHES *and* TRUNKFISHES

This bizarre family is related to the pufferfishes and the fishes' most striking feature is the hard "shell" that encases their entire bodies except for the mouth, eyes, fins and gill openings. They move around using sculling motions rather than swimming like other fishes and their fins reflect this, being reduced in size, broad and paddle-like. They are very slow swimmers, but can put on a spurt if they need to by lashing their comparatively large tails from side to side. Mostly, they lead quiet lives close to the bottom, secure in the knowledge that their hard shell makes them safe from attack. However, when they are higher in the water they become more vulnerable because the armor doesn't extend to their belly parts, which are just like any other fish's. Any attack made from below will result in a wound that sometimes becomes infected. When they are attacked – and sometimes when they are dying – some members of this family can emit a toxic substance that not only kills everything else in the aquarium but also themselves in a very short time. It is thought that the mechanism for this was evolved to deter predators, as the toxin glands are near the mouth and the favorite way for predators to attack is from the front.

The family is distributed worldwide, being common in some areas. There are less than 50 valid species, mostly less than 30 cm (12 in) long, although some

species grow to twice that length. They make excellent additions to any quiet aquarium devoid of boisterous species or bullies. Their slow movements seem to attract *Labroides dimidiatus* (Cleaner Wrasses), but they appear to resent the attentions of those well-meaning little fishes. They quickly suffer the effects of starvation, so avoid specimens that have a sunken appearance. Feed them regularly – they particularly enjoy live food.

Ostracion
Perhaps the cutest family in the hobby.

Lactoria cornuta
Interesting to look at and a great favorite.

KEY

LENGTH IN WILD (IN)	
LENGTH IN CAPTIVITY (IN)	
HERBIVORE	
OMNIVORE	
PREDATOR	
SINGLE SPECIMEN	
COMMUNITY FISH	
SAFE WITH SMALL FISHES	
SAFE WITH INVERTEBRATES	
EASE OF KEEPING FOR BEGINNERS (SCALE OF 1–10)	7

LACTORIA CORNUTA
COWFISH

This appealing Indo-Pacific species has two horns on the head and two more at the rear of its body, just below the tail. While these add to its appeal, they can become a source of infection should one become damaged in a scuffle, so only quiet, peaceful species should be kept in its aquarium. This species – and any of its relatives – should always be first into a tank to avoid causing undue stress. The cautionary note refers to the fact that specimens kept together can sometimes quarrel among themselves. This species will eat any aquarium food but likes to browse on algae and enjoys live brine shrimps.

Ostracion meleagris
This species is prone to bacterial infections of the skin.

OSTRACION MELEAGRIS
SPOTTED BOXFISH

Although this striking species can be kept easily by an experienced aquarist, it is not for the beginner because it is very susceptible to bacterial infections of the skin and, more commonly, the eyes. This Indo-Pacific species was once thought to be hermaphrodite – changing sex as required – but the remarkable color variation is between male and female forms. The female is all black with white spots, but the male has violet flanks with yellow spots and a black top with white spots. More than any of its cousins, this species needs absolutely perfect water quality if it is to flourish. All other care factors are the same as for other members of the group.

KEY

 LENGTH IN
WILD (IN)

 LENGTH IN
CAPTIVITY (IN)

 HERBIVORE

 OMNIVORE

 PREDATOR

 SINGLE SPECIMEN

 COMMUNITY FISH

 SAFE WITH
SMALL FISHES

 SAFE WITH
INVERTEBRATES

 7 EASE OF KEEPING
FOR BEGINNERS
(SCALE OF 1–10)

TETROSOMUS GIBBOSUS

HOVERCRAFTFISH

 **6**

This species, from the Indo-Pacific as far west as the Red Sea to as far east as Japan, is aptly named because it seems to hover in mid-water. Although peaceful, it will quarrel with its own kind in captivity. It will also destroy many invertebrates. That said, it makes an engaging aquarium fish. It is distinguished from others in the family by the high pointed ridge on its back, which ends in a blunt, compressed spine. It also has a pair of spines on the head, although they are nowhere near as pointed as in *Lactoria cornuta*. It also carries five blunt, curved spines along the lower ridge of the body and because of these it should never be caught in a net. The need for quiet tankmates is even more important than with other boxfishes because it can be a target for fin-nipping species. Like *O. meleagris*, it loves live foods.

**Tetrosomus
gibbosus**
Although peaceful, this
species will fight with
its own kind in captivity.

Q I keep a Hovercraftfish (*Tetrosomus gibbosus*) which always seems to have a scrappy underside. The skin on its stomach looks ragged and there are sometimes open wounds which, thankfully, have healed up to now. What causes this and how can I prevent it?

A Although armor-plated, Hovercraft have unprotected undersides. Another fish in your tank is attacking it, so either take out the aggressor or the Hovercraft. Meanwhile, make sure that the wounds do not become sites for secondary infections, like fungus.

*P*LATACIDAE

BATFISHES

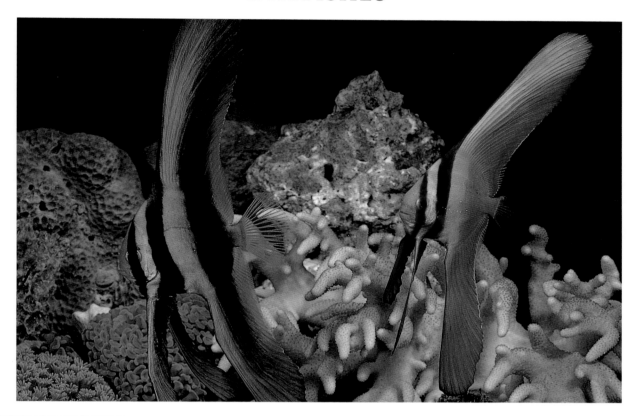

With the advent and subsequent popularity of reef-type aquaria, batfishes have declined in popularity. This is a pity, because there can be no more stately, friendly or attractive group of fishes. They are found in coastal – sometimes brackish – waters and in mangrove swamps. Their chief behavioral characteristic is that of playing dead when attacked, by lying on their sides to look like leaves. They also do this when first introduced into an aquarium, provoking panic in their new owners. Batfishes need a large deep tank because they grow very large, very quickly and also have very large dorsal and anal fins. It pays to buy only juvenile specimens that you know to be feeding. Adult fishes may prove impossible to acclimatize to aquarium foods. Once they are acclimatized, however, they will eat any aquarium food – they are particularly fond of earthworms – and harm nothing.

Platacidae
Because they grow so big, this family is for large aquariums only.

KEY

 LENGTH IN WILD (IN)

 LENGTH IN CAPTIVITY (IN)

 HERBIVORE

 OMNIVORE

 PREDATOR

 SINGLE SPECIMEN

 COMMUNITY FISH

 SAFE WITH SMALL FISHES

 SAFE WITH INVERTEBRATES

 EASE OF KEEPING FOR BEGINNERS (SCALE OF 1–10)

PLATAX ORBICULARIS

ORBICULATE BATFISH

*T*his is the most common of the batfishes, and so is the one most frequently seen in captivity. It is found in the Indo-Pacific, being abundant in the Eastern Pacific, where it scavenges around for whatever it can get to eat. Provided it has a deep tank with plenty of swimming space, and there are no bullies or species to nip its delicate fins, this species will live for years.

Platax orbicularis
Keep this species well away from potential fin-nippers.

PLATAX PINNATUS

RED-FINNED BATFISH

*U*nlike *P. orbicularis*, this fish is somewhat delicate and can never be recommended to beginners. However, an aquarist with a year or two's experience should be able to provide the excellent water quality it needs and be able to get it feeding – something that the novice could find impossible. The body is much smaller than that of *P. orbicularis* and the fins are elongated. It is also much darker, and outlined with red. This species will relish live food, and live brine shrimps usually tempt it to feed.

Platax pinnatus
Pretty delicate when compared with the species above.

PLECTORHYNCHIDAE

SWEETLIPS

Depending on which authority you read, this family is sometimes classified with the Pomadasyidae and sometimes with the Haemulidae. The sweetlips stand alone, however, because of their dental arrangements, and are generally acknowledged as a family in their own right. All members come from the Indo-Pacific region, where they live mostly in shallow water, being very abundant on coral reefs. They sometimes form large, loose schools containing hundreds of individuals. Sweetlips are an important food fish in some areas, although not as important as their close cousins, the snappers (Lutjanidae).

The sweetlips do well in captivity on the whole, being completely indifferent to other species. However, they are not the strongest of species and so only quiet tankmates should be housed with them. They should not be kept with invertebrates as they can become destructive towards them as they mature. Feed them a varied diet of all the usual aquarium foods. Coloration will change remarkably with age.

Plectorhynchidae
The members of this group are close cousins of the snappers.

Q I have a Yellow-lined Sweetlips which I bought two years ago. It is fine, except that it has been gradually losing its color over the past two to three months. What could be causing this?

A Don't worry. This is natural. The Yellow-lined Sweetlips changes color as it matures and that is precisely what is happening. I should tell you, however, that your fish will become a very dull brown color eventually.

PLECTORHYNCHUS ALBOVITTATUS

YELLOW-LINED SWEETLIPS

Plectorhynchus albovittatus

The brilliant coloring of this species fades with age.

*B*eing mainly yellow, with two brown bars running the whole length of their body, the juveniles of this species are very attractive. However, this coloring fades as the fish matures and the adults become a very dull brown. A large aquarium housing quiet species is a prerequisite, as it becomes very shy in the company of more boisterous tankmates and if faced with them will probably die of starvation. Kept with the correct species, however, it is as hardy as any other. Feed it on small crustaceans – brine shrimps are ideal – and other meaty foods.

Plectorhynchus chaetodonoides
The alternative common name of this species – the Polka-dot Grunt – seems very apt.

KEY

LENGTH IN WILD (IN)	
LENGTH IN CAPTIVITY (IN)	
HERBIVORE	
OMNIVORE	
PREDATOR	
SINGLE SPECIMEN	
COMMUNITY FISH	
SAFE WITH SMALL FISHES	
SAFE WITH INVERTEBRATES	
EASE OF KEEPING FOR BEGINNERS (SCALE OF 1–10)	

PLECTORHYNCHUS CHAETODONOIDES

HARLEQUIN SWEETLIPS

Sometimes sold as the Polka-dot Grunt, this species is probably the most frequently seen sweetlips within the hobby. The juveniles are very striking, being dark brown and covered with white blotches, these blotches being carried over onto the fins. The adults, by comparison, are very drab. The Harlequin Sweetlips, more than any other, can be very shy and needs a quiet home away from bullies and boisterous species in order to thrive. Given these tranquil surroundings, it will live long and happily, feeding on any small aquarium fare, and particularly relishing live brine shrimps. It will also relish many invertebrates as it matures, so it should never be considered for an invertebrate aquarium.

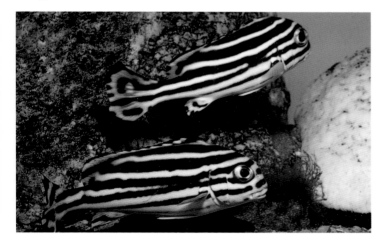

Plectorhynchus orientalis
Tends to be extremely fragile in captivity, so not recommended for beginners.

PLECTORHYNCHUS ORIENTALIS

ORIENTAL SWEETLIPS

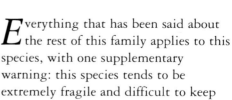

Everything that has been said about the rest of this family applies to this species, with one supplementary warning: this species tends to be extremely fragile and difficult to keep for any length of time in captivity. The specimen shown here is a juvenile. The adult looks something like the juvenile *P. albovittatus*.

PLOTOSIDAE

CATFISHES

There is only one member of this family of any interest to the aquarium hobby, and even it is of limited appeal. This is a small family of catfishes, most members of which are marine, or at least estuarine, although a couple of species live in freshwater. They are all elongated, with scaleless bodies whose first dorsal fin is set just behind the head. The first ray of this fin is a strong spine. A second dorsal fin is continuous with the tail and anal fins, and the pectoral fins have a sharp spine and several rays. These spines, along with the one on the dorsal fin, are venomous. Barbels around the mouth are used for locating food as the fish grubs along the bottom. The family is confined to the Indo-Pacific area.

Plotosidae

Only one member of this family is of interest to the aquarium hobby.

106

KEY

LENGTH IN
WILD (IN)

LENGTH IN
CAPTIVITY (IN)

HERBIVORE

OMNIVORE

PREDATOR

SINGLE SPECIMEN

COMMUNITY FISH

SAFE WITH
SMALL FISHES

SAFE WITH
INVERTEBRATES

EASE OF KEEPING
FOR BEGINNERS
(SCALE OF 1–10)

Plotosus lineatus
When kept in small groups, this species will perform its trick of rolling around the aquarium.

PLOTOSUS LINEATUS

MARINE CATFISH

*T*his species is difficult to keep because it has venomous spines and needs to be handled with care. Although it is handsome when young, it loses its distinctive stripes and becomes very dowdy as an adult. It is well known, when young, for schooling in tightly-knit groups that form into a ball – providing protection against predators.

Plotosus lineatus is widely distributed throughout the Indo-Pacific, from East Africa to South-east Asia. In South Africa, it is considered good to eat, although it is not eaten anywhere else. This species could be kept in brackish or wholly freshwater aquariums if properly acclimatized, since in the wild it frequently enters river systems. In the aquarium this species should be fed on chopped, meaty foods, mussels being a favorite. It should be kept in small groups as lone specimens seem to pine. It grows very quickly and will need to be moved to larger quarters at some point.

Q I have a Marine Catfish (*Plotosus lineatus*) which doesn't seem to be doing very well. In fact, I hardly see it feeding. What can I do?

A *Plotosus lineatus* never does very well when kept alone. You have to buy another three or four specimens, but this could be difficult if the one that you already have is established. Although you say that you hardly see it feeding, as long as it hasn't gone too far, it should be fine when others of its own kind are around.

POMACANTHIDAE

ANGELFISHES

*T*his large family of wonderful fishes, with members strewn across the world, is probably the most popular of all with marine aquarists. The family used to be classified with the Chaetodontidae – the butterflyfishes – but can be distinguished from them by the spines on its gill covers, a feature that is missing in the butterflyfishes. Angelfishes have a minority group within their ranks, however – the Dwarf or *Centropyge* angels. While the family has members that can grow to 61 cm (24 in) long, the dwarf angels rarely exceed 10 cm (4 in). However, *Centropyge* species are true angelfishes and are included here.

As mentioned earlier, the family is well represented all over the world, in tropical and warm temperate seas. They are colorful, somewhat deep-bodied fish and many of the family – but not the *Centropyge* species – have a different

Pomacanthidae
Probably the most popular family of all with marine aquarists.

LENGTH IN WILD (IN)

LENGTH IN CAPTIVITY (IN)

HERBIVORE

OMNIVORE

PREDATOR

SINGLE SPECIMEN

COMMUNITY FISH

SAFE WITH SMALL FISHES

SAFE WITH INVERTEBRATES

EASE OF KEEPING FOR BEGINNERS (SCALE OF 1–10) 7

color, pattern or both, when juveniles. As juveniles, many species are known to clean parasites from other species, and it is thought that the usual juvenile color patterns are advertisements for this service, deterring predators or aggressive adults of the same species. Spawning is carried out by one male and one female swimming upwards through the water column, scattering eggs and sperm at the same time. The eggs, and later the fry, are left to take their chances in the plankton, the fry staying there for around a month, after which they drop to the seabed. The adults play no further part in parenting after producing and fertilizing the eggs.

As a general rule, angelfishes of the same or similar species should not be kept together in the aquarium. These beasts are very territorial and will defend their space to the death. Having said that, there are exceptions to this rule. If you must keep two angelfishes together, naturally the aquarium should be large enough to house them. They should also be of a different genus – for example, you could get away with keeping one *Pomacanthus* species in the same tank as one *Holocanthus* species – unless, of course, you are lucky enough to get a mated pair.

In the wild, sponges make up a large part of an angelfish's diet, but it is out of the question to feed these in captivity. For this reason, it is suggested that only juveniles be purchased as they will acclimatize more easily. Having said that, sponge-based frozen foods are now available and you should try to obtain

them if possible. Even a specimen bought as a juvenile and fully acclimatized to an aquarium diet will relish a weekly feed on this delicacy. Excellent water quality is needed, and a good algae growth is mandatory since all species are extremely susceptible to deteriorating water quality. When they are not eating sponges, they spend a large part of their time browsing over the reef on algae. For these reasons, angelfishes are not recommended for beginners.

Q I love large angelfishes and would like very much to keep more than one. Is this possible? I have a 450 l (100 gal) aquarium.

A First, you have to consider your stocking level. For the sake of this question, we will assume that you have enough space. You can get away with two large angelfishes, provided that you buy two which are of different sizes, as different in colour as possible and are from different genera. For instance, you could get one *Pomacanthus* species to live happily with a *Holocanthus* species.

KEY

 LENGTH IN WILD (IN)

 LENGTH IN CAPTIVITY (IN)

 HERBIVORE

 OMNIVORE

 PREDATOR

 SINGLE SPECIMEN

 COMMUNITY FISH

 SAFE WITH SMALL FISHES

 SAFE WITH INVERTEBRATES

 EASE OF KEEPING FOR BEGINNERS (SCALE OF 1–10)

Arusetta asfur
Often confused with *Pomacanthus maculosus*, this species can be differentiated by the incomplete yellow crescent.

ARUSETTA ASFUR

HALF-MOON ANGELFISH

This species usually comes into the trade from the Red Sea, but is also found in the Indo-Pacific. It is highly prized by aquarists, and so *Arusetta asfur* commands a high price. The species *Pomacanthus maculosus* looks very similar to this species, but can be distinguished by the yellow crescent on the flanks. On *A. asfur*, the crescent ends about two-thirds of the way down the side, whereas on *P. maculosus* it extends into the anal fin.

This species can be delicate in captivity, so should only be considered by aquarists with lots of experience in feeding and water management. However, in the right hands, acclimatized and provided with first-class water, *A. asfur* will do well when fed on all of the usual aquarium fare.

EUXIPHIPOPS NAVARCHUS

MAJESTIC ANGELFISH

*T*his species is much hardier in captivity than the previous one, although it is still comparatively delicate and is not for beginners. Compared to other members of the family, however, it is relatively long-lived and strong provided that all the rules are adhered to. This Pacific species is also highly sought after and, because of this, is also usually expensive. It is, however, a truly striking beast that, in the hands of an experienced aquarist, will live for years. Individuals of this species relish shellfish and other meaty foods and will also spend many daylight hours browsing on algae. Top-quality water is essential.

Euxiphipops navarchus

Only top-quality water conditions will suffice for this beauty.

Euxiphipops xanthometapon

Plenty of experience will be needed before the hobbyist can hope to be able to provide the high levels of care needed for this species.

EUXIPHIPOPS XANTHOMETAPON

BLUE-FACED ANGELFISH

*T*he hobby is undecided on whether this Indo-Pacific species should be called the Blue-faced or the Yellow-faced Angelfish so, as with many coralfish species, it is always safer to use scientific names. Whatever it is called, it is a wonderful beast, somewhat difficult to keep, so should never be considered by beginners. Its keeper will need plenty of experience in order to provide the high degree of care needed to keep it happy. Once happy, though, this beauty will live for years. Everything regarding care and feeding for the previous species also applies here.

HOLOCANTHUS CILIARIS

QUEEN ANGELFISH

*T*his Western Atlantic species, which is found around Bermuda and as far south as Brazil, is one of the jewels of the seawater aquarium. It thrives in captivity provided that its natural lifestyle is taken into account. There should be plenty of swimming space in the aquarium, together with places into which it can retire at night. There should be a good growth of algae available to it, and the quality of the water must be second to none. It should be fed a varied diet, with sponge-based food playing a significant part. This species can become very aggressive with age, and menacing toward invertebrates.

It is remarkably similar to *Holocanthus bermudensis*, its close relative, which has straighter blue lines on its body than *H. ciliaris* in the juvenile stage. Hybrids are known to occur between the two species.

Holocanthus ciliaris

Only an aquarium of regal proportions will be good enough for the queen.

Holocanthus passer

One of the most aggressive species of all.

HOLOCANTHUS PASSER

KING ANGELFISH

*L*ike *H. ciliaris*, *Holocanthus passer* fully justifies its common name, King Angelfish. It is found in the Pacific Ocean, where it lives on the reef, singly or in pairs. This species is equally as strong as *H. ciliaris* in the aquarium. It is also one of the most aggressive species ever likely to grace an aquarium, so great care should be taken when selecting species to share its home. It is, however, a very satisfying species to keep. It will eat any aquarium food, once acclimatized, and seems very resistant to disease.

Pomacanthus imperator

In a family of favorites, this is probably the favorite of them all.

KEY

LENGTH IN WILD (IN)

LENGTH IN CAPTIVITY (IN)

HERBIVORE

OMNIVORE

PREDATOR

SINGLE SPECIMEN

COMMUNITY FISH

SAFE WITH SMALL FISHES

SAFE WITH INVERTEBRATES

EASE OF KEEPING FOR BEGINNERS (SCALE OF 1–10) 7

POMACANTHUS IMPERATOR

EMPEROR ANGELFISH

◄ 16 ► | ◄ 10 ► | | | | | 8

*I*n a family of aquarium favorites, this is probably the favorite of them all. Ask most aquarists which fish they most aspire to keep and the answer would probably be, "the Emperor Angelfish."

One look will tell you why. This Indo-Pacific beauty's garish colors and pattern camouflage it on the reef, where it blends in with all the colored sponges, corals and anemones to become almost invisible. *Pomacanthus imperator* is a comparatively hardy species in captivity, although inexperienced aquarists should avoid it for the first year or two. It will feed happily on all the usual aquarium foods, but is particularly fond of shellfish.

Pygoplytes diacanthus

Only specimens from the Red Sea or the Maldives and Sri Lanka are likely to succeed.

PYGOPLYTES DIACANTHUS

REGAL ANGELFISH

◄ 10 ► | ◄ 6-7 ► | | | | | 5

*T*his species is not for the beginner as it can prove difficult to acclimatize. More than with any other species, water quality needs to be perfect or that fabulous coloration will fade and the animal refuse to eat. Regal Angelfish from some areas can be very pale and are the worst to persuade to feed. However, specimens from the Red Sea, the Maldives or Sri Lanka will provide a better chance as they will usually feed given good conditions, patience and a variety of items. Sponge-based foods and a good growth of algae in the aquarium will help.

KEY

 LENGTH IN WILD (IN)

 LENGTH IN CAPTIVITY (IN)

 HERBIVORE

 OMNIVORE

 PREDATOR

 SINGLE SPECIMEN

 COMMUNITY FISH

 SAFE WITH SMALL FISHES

 SAFE WITH INVERTEBRATES

 7 EASE OF KEEPING FOR BEGINNERS (SCALE OF 1–10)

Centropyge bicolor
Once considered difficult, provided that its natural requirements are taken into account, this species will provide years of fishkeeping pleasure.

CENTROPYGE BICOLOR

BICOLOR ANGELFISH

*E*ven though this – the most striking of all *Centropyge* species – could never be recommended to newcomers to the hobby, it should pose no problems for a fishkeeper with a few months' experience. *Centropyge bicolor* used to be considered difficult to keep, but more is known about it now. In the wild, this species lives primarily over areas of rubble and coral debris, and it is a good idea to replicate this as closely as possible in captivity. There should be plenty of swimming space, but also hideouts into which it can retreat at night. It likes to eat small, meaty foods, but is also very fond of algae, so a good growth of this should be attempted in the aquarium. As with all *Centropyge* species, it is usually fine in invertebrate aquariums.

Q I would really love to try spawning the Dwarf Angelfish, *Centropyge bicolor*. I know that two will fight, so how do I go about getting a pair?

A The best way is to buy a group of five or six and let them pair off naturally. When they do, you will have to find new homes for the others.

CENTROPYGE BISPINOSUS

CORAL BEAUTY

This aptly-named species comes from the coral reefs of the Indo-Pacific, from South Africa in the west, as far east as Tahiti in the Western Pacific. It is very abundant over the Great Barrier Reef, where it lives in drop-offs, and the Philippines. Specimens from this latter region are a very much deeper blue/red than individuals caught elsewhere. Indeed, the coloration of the species can vary so much – depending on where they came from – that the untrained eye could easily mistake two specimens of *C. bispinosus* for two different species.

It is very shy both in the wild and in captivity. In order to thrive, it needs plenty of hiding places to retreat into when it feels threatened. In fact, the more hiding places there are, the less it will use them. *Centropyge bispinosus* spends much of its day browsing on algae and appreciates it in the aquarium. Other foods to include in its diet are brine shrimps and the occasional meal of bloodworms.

Centropyge bispinosus

Plenty of hiding places will make the difference between a shy, retiring specimen and a bold, showy one.

CENTROPYGE FLAVISSIMUS

LEMON-PEEL ANGELFISH

*B*eing found around the islands of the Central Pacific, this species is by far the most common member of its family in that area. It is a shallow-water species that lives on a diet predominantly of algae, supplementing this with small crustaceans and worms. The juveniles look very much like adults, except that young males have a black spot on their sides. This black spot – which is ringed in blue – disappears as the fish matures. In the past, this species was considered difficult to keep, but for some reason they have shed that label and are often kept with much success. There is a very closely related, almost identical, species called *C. heraldi* (Herald Angelfish). The two can be told apart, however, by the distinctive blue ring around the eye of *C. flavissimus*.

Although this species has been kept in considerable numbers with success, it will only thrive in superb water and in an aquarium with plenty of algae. It should also be offered foods such as brine shrimps. This species does best in an invertebrate aquarium, away from bullies.

Q I bought what I thought was a Lemon-peel Angelfish recently. I was happy with my purchase until a fellow fishkeeper came to my house and said it was a Herald Angel.

A *Centropyge flavissimus* (Lemon-peel Angelfish) and *C. heraldi* (Herald Angelfish) look very much alike and the novice could have problems telling them apart. However, if yours is *C. flavissimus* it will have a blue ring around each eye. If you have *C. heraldi*, don't worry; both are equally attractive and care for both should be identical.

Centropyge flavissimus
This species is best in a quiet invertebrate aquarium.

**Centropyge
loriculus**
Possibly the hardiest
species in the family –
certainly the most
expensive.

CENTROPYGE
LORICULUS

FLAME ANGELFISH

This species is another favorite with marine aquarists. There are two reasons for this. One is its undeniable beauty. The other is that it is, possibly, the hardiest member of its family. There is also a drawback, however. Because its natural habitat is the outer reef slopes – at depths as great as 25 m (85 ft) – it is very expensive compared to other Centropyge species. However, this hasn't deterred the world's fishkeepers because it is a truly wonderful species that graces any fish collection. Being found scattered around the Western Pacific, where it is never common (another reason for its high price), most specimens come into the trade via Hawaii, one of the best sources of aquarium fishes.

The above are just a few of the angelfish species available to the hobbyist. Space dictates that details cannot be given for more, but additional species that can be recommended to the beginner or aquarist with limited experience are: *Pomacanthus semicirculatus, P. paru, P. annularis, Holocanthus bermudensis, Centropyge vroliki, C. eibli* and *C. argi.* Please also refer to the list of species to be avoided (page 153).

POMACENTRIDAE

DAMSELFISHES *and* ANEMONEFISHES

*T*wenty years ago, when the seawater aquarium was a new hobby, this huge family was easily the most popular group. Things have progressed to such an extent that all manner of species are now kept, even those once considered impossible, and it says a lot about the appeal of this family that it is still immensely popular.

A large family of mainly small, usually colorful fishes, this group is represented all around the world, on tropical coral reefs and in warmer temperate seas. It is a family of somewhat deep-bodied fishes with a single nostril on each side of the head.

Damselfishes live on the world's coral reefs, and are usually found around the coral, where they wait for food to come along in the current and dash into the coral heads whenever danger threatens. This group is extremely hardy and were traditionally used to mature filters. However, this does not make good fishkeeping sense for two principle

Pomacentridae
This is the family which probably started it all for most marine aquarists.

reasons. The high ammonia and nitrite levels that accompany an immature filter cause this species as much stress as any other (see page 24). Secondly, as damselfishes mature, they invariably become aggressive, causing problems with the selection of other species to add to the aquarium at a later stage. It is far better to look on these fishes as hardy species to keep if you lack experience.

There are lots of damselfish species that look so alike that they make identification very difficult – even among experts. However, this is not really important because members of the family mostly behave in the same manner and are kept equally easily. The damselfishes have provided plenty of spawning successes in the past, laying their eggs over a pre-prepared site and the male parent guarding the eggs until they hatch. On the whole, damselfishes are straightforward to keep, being easily pleased with regard to food and relatively insensitive to deteriorating water quality.

Anemonefishes – also called clownfishes due to their vivid colors – are famous for their symbiotic/commensal association with anemones, mainly those of the genus *Stoichactis*, but sometimes others too. Whereas most fish that swim too close to an anemone would be paralyzed by the stinging cells within its tentacles (properly called nematocysts), the anemonefish lives happily within its tentacles, thereby gaining protection from predators while providing the anemone with food in return. Why the Anemonefish is

immune to the anemone's sting is still a matter of debate. The old school of thought, which still has its followers, says that the fish must earn its immunity by carefully rubbing itself against the anemone's tentacles. A more modern argument – favored by most authorities – is that it is covered by a polysaccharine coating that the anemone doesn't recognize as being of animal origin. However, this does not explain the fact that an anemonefish that has been deprived of an anemone for a while appears to have to "re-immunize" itself when the anemone is reintroduced. Nor does it explain why some species of damselfish – particularly the Domino Damselfish – can also gain immunity and are regularly seen swimming in and out of anemone tentacles.

In the aquarium, an anemonefish/anemone partnership makes a wonderful centerpiece, and will be a talking point among fellow enthusiasts. Anemonefish, by and large, make good aquarium subjects – although not all are as tough as some authorities would have us believe. They are happy to eat all of the usual aquarium foods, however, including flake food. Anemonefishes breed in larger quantities in captivity than do any other family.

KEY

 LENGTH IN WILD (IN)

 LENGTH IN CAPTIVITY (IN)

 HERBIVORE

 OMNIVORE

 PREDATOR

 SINGLE SPECIMEN

 COMMUNITY FISH

 SAFE WITH SMALL FISHES

 SAFE WITH INVERTEBRATES

 EASE OF KEEPING FOR BEGINNERS (SCALE OF 1–10)

Abudefduf cyaneus
A superb aquarium subject, being hardy and long-lived.

ABUDEFDUF CYANEUS

BLUE DAMSELFISH

    8

This Indo-Pacific species is extremely common on the reefs around the Philippines, Samoa and other islands of the Western Pacific. It should be kept singly or in shoals of around six, since it becomes very pugnacious and will squabble with its own kind. There are so many other species that look like this one that even a trained eye can get confused. However, they all make terrific aquarium additions, being very hardy and relatively long-lived.

Abudefduf oxydon
The "neon" pattern which gives this species its common name will disappear with age.

ABUDEFDUF OXYDON

NEON DAMSELFISH

     6

One look at its remarkable appearance will tell you why this fish got its common name: the blue flashes on the pitch-black body look just like neon lights against a dark night sky. However, these flashes will disappear as the fish matures. Being found in the Pacific Ocean, this species demands more from the aquarist in terms of water quality than do the rest of its family. It is also very aggressive and should be kept alone as conspecifics will be treated unmercifully. This species likes to eat algae and small meaty foods.

ABUDEFDUF SAXATILIS

SARGEANT MAJOR

This species is extremely common throughout tropical oceans and is an exception to the rule in this aggressive family. In fact, because it can grow comparatively large, the size of the aquarium is the only limitation on the number that can be kept together. In the main, this species will pose no threat to anything else in the aquarium and so makes an ideal choice, especially since it is so tough. Like the other *Abudefduf* species, this is a plankton-feeder that also feeds on algae. In the confines of the aquarium, this means that it will eat any aquarium food. Indeed, it is this species that flocks around tourist boats, waiting for bread or other human food items to fall overboard.

Abudefduf saxatilis
Far less pugnacious than other members of its family.

Amphiprion clarkii
This clownfish can live very happily without a host anemone.

AMPHIPRION CLARKII

CLARK'S ANEMONEFISH

This common Indo-Pacific species is something of an enigma. It is extremely hardy, generally peaceful and makes a good community fish that can live very happily without a host anemone. However, some individuals – especially when kept singly with an anemone – can become brutes as they mature. Having said that, a pair with an anemone is usually peaceful. Then again, a pair without an anemone can be very pugnacious – even to each other, which is probably due to the fact that it is difficult to achieve a sexual bond without a central focal point for the two. This species is also very closely related to *A. sebae* and looks so similar that it is difficult to tell the two apart. Indeed, some authorities believe that they are, in fact, the same species. In any case, they are both hardy, long-lived fishes that will eat any aquarium food.

AMPHIPRION FRENATUS

TOMATO CLOWNFISH

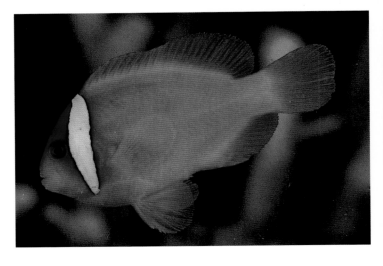

Coming from the Pacific Ocean — around the islands to the west — this species is sometimes called *A. melanopus*. This is also a species with a close cousin, *A. ephippium*, that looks very similar and also has the common name Tomato Clownfish. The two differ in that, while the white stripe stays with *A. frenatus*, *A. ephippium* loses it as it matures. This species can become very aggressive with age so should be added last to a community. However, it can be an excellent choice for the beginner since it is very hardy, undemanding about food, and will be very happy without an anemone.

Amphiprion frenatus

One of two species with the common name of Tomato Clownfish.

Amphiprion ocellaris

Pictures of this species with their host anemones are seen all over the world.

AMPHIPRION OCELLARIS

COMMON CLOWNFISH

Pictures of Common Clownfishes in their anemone are seen all over the world and are probably the reason why most marine aquarists start the hobby.

Once again. *A. ocellaris* has a very close, almost identical relative in *A. percula*. The two are so similar that there is much disagreement about whether they are simply color variations of the same species. *Amphiprion ocellaris* tends to be a much paler orange, and is much easier to keep than *A. percula*, which can be extremely delicate. However, this species will do well as long as it has a host anemone and a partner. Single specimens have a tendency not to do well, especially without an anemone. It needs to be fed small or finely chopped foods: brine shrimps, bloodworms and chopped mussels. It may also have to be tempted to eat dried and flake food. This species has spawned and been raised in captivity more successfully than any other, and many tank-bred specimens are found in the stores. It is possible to join the ranks of captive breeders if suitable rocks are provided on which they can lay their eggs.

Amphiprion perideraion
If this species is to thrive, a host anemone is mandatory.

KEY

 LENGTH IN WILD (IN)

 LENGTH IN CAPTIVITY (IN)

 HERBIVORE

 OMNIVORE

 PREDATOR

 SINGLE SPECIMEN

 COMMUNITY FISH

 SAFE WITH SMALL FISHES

SAFE WITH INVERTEBRATES

EASE OF KEEPING FOR BEGINNERS (SCALE OF 1–10) 7

AMPHIPRION PERIDERAION

PINK SKUNK CLOWNFISH

 3½ | 2 | 5

This quiet little species from the Pacific Ocean definitely requires a host anemone to stand even a chance of aquarium survival. It is much more sensitive than any other anemonefish and does best in an invertebrate aquarium, well away from any boisterous species. Feeding should be achieved using small or chopped meaty foods. This is another species with a close cousin, *A. akallopisos*, that looks very similar, except that the latter lacks the white bar of *A perideraion*.

POMACENTRUS VIOLASCENS

YELLOW-TAILED BLUE DAMSELFISH

 3 | 1½ | 7

Another Pacific species, this is probably the most commonly kept damselfish. It will fare very well in captivity, but has to be kept in groups, as it can become pugnacious if kept singly or in pairs. A plankton-feeder, it does well when fed small food items such as brine shrimps. The Domino and the Humbug are also common damselfishes. Very hardy, they are ideal for beginners but, like the Yellow-tailed Blue, they can become very aggressive when they grow.

Pomacentrus violascens
This damselfish should be kept in groups, as it becomes pugnacious when alone or in pairs.

PSEUDOCHROMIDAE

DOTTYBACKS

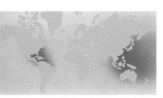

This family of small, colorful reef fishes from the Indo-Pacific are the counterparts of the Grammidae from the Caribbean. Indeed, they are seen by some as the "poor man's grammas," and one species – *Pseudochromis paccagnellae* – is even called the False Gramma. This seems a little unfair, as these fishes are attractive and interesting enough in their own right. In fact, they are heaven-sent fishes for the invertebrate or very quiet, fish-only aquarium, being small, colorful, hardy and in the main part peaceful. They are slender-bodied, with a long-based dorsal fin that has only three spines, a characteristic that distinguishes them from the *Serranidae* family, to which both they and the grammas are allied.

Although they are shy, dottybacks are extremely territorial. In the wild they spend long hours swimming in the crevices on the reef, darting out now and again to catch any food item that gets swept past in the current. They will carry this behavior over into the aquarium, lying up in caves and crevices in the rockwork for most of the day, then darting out to catch food. However, they also have a tendency to dash out and nip passing tankmates – an unwelcome trait that has earned them a reputation for aggression.

They settle into aquarium life very well and lose their inhibitions very quickly. They need plenty of places in which to hide so that they can settle in

and live a normal life. They should be offered small food items and particularly relish live brine shrimps.

KEY

LENGTH IN WILD (IN)

LENGTH IN CAPTIVITY (IN)

HERBIVORE

OMNIVORE

PREDATOR

SINGLE SPECIMEN

COMMUNITY FISH

SAFE WITH SMALL FISHES

SAFE WITH INVERTEBRATES

EASE OF KEEPING FOR BEGINNERS (SCALE OF 1–10)   7

Pseudochromidae

The Indo-Pacific counterparts of the Grammidae, which come from the Caribbean.

PSEUDOCHROMIS DIADEMA

FLASH-BACK DOTTYBACK

Pseudochromis diadema

Becoming popular with aquarists after years in the doldrums.

This striking species, found in the Western Pacific, seems to be becoming popular with marine aquarists after a long time in the shadow of other, similar species. Provided that it has a plethora of hiding places at its disposal, this species will settle in well and prove to be extremely long-lived. However, it will attack members of its own or any similar species, so must be kept alone in the aquarium. Even bearing this in mind, however, *P. diadema* is an excellent choice for the beginner, being hardy and easy to feed. It will take most suitably sized frozen or live foods, as well as flake food.

Pseudochromis paccagnellae
Called the False Gramma because of its similarity to that species.

PSEUDOCHROMIS PACCAGNELLAE
FALSE GRAMMA

Often also referred to as Paccagnella's Dottyback, this Pacific Ocean species looks so like *Gramma loreto* (Royal Gramma) from the Caribbean, that the beginner could be forgiven for confusing the two species. However, they are very easily distinguished by the white line that divides the purple head region from the yellow posterior half of

P. paccagnellae. The *G. loreto* also has a black spot on its dorsal fin and a black line through the eye, and *P. paccagnellae* lacks both of these.

In the aquarium, *P. paccagnellae* should be treated like all members of its family: it should be kept well away from members of its own family or similar species, should have plenty of hiding places and be fed with small, meaty foods. Warning! This species will nip at the fins of other species, especially if they have long fins or are slow swimmers. It is, however, a hardy and relatively peaceful species.

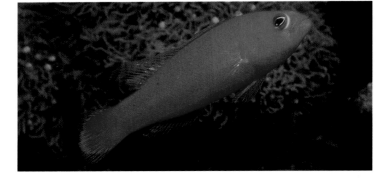

Pseudochromis porphyreus
This species is a beginner's dream.

PSEUDOCHROMIS PORPHYREUS
STRAWBERRYFISH

This lovely little fish is misnamed, being purple rather than red. It is a beginner's dream. Easy to feed and very tough in captivity, it makes a striking addition to any collection. It is also very bold – too bold in many respects, for it will attack anything that looks remotely like itself. Indeed, any fish that it simply dislikes, of whatever size, color or pattern, could come in for some rough treatment. This should not deter you, though, because it is a handsome species.

SCATOPHAGIDAE

SCATS

Unlike all the other species in this book, the species in this family – which number four, only one of which is of any importance to the aquarium hobby – will thrive in fresh, brackish or sea water. This is because they live in estuaries in their native countries (see also the catfishes). They are all found in the Indo-Pacific region, from East Africa, throughout the Indian Ocean as far as the Western Pacific islands. They have a well-developed, spiny dorsal fin that is separate from a soft, second dorsal fin behind. The anal fin has four spines, each one covered in tiny scales.

Scatophagidae
The scats will do equally well in fresh or brackish water.

Scatophagus argus
As with so many species, the adult is very plain in comparison with the juvenile fish.

SCATOPHAGUS ARGUS

SCAT

This species has a tendency to swarm around sewage outfalls in the wild. Indeed, "scatophagus," literally translated, means dung-eater. Juvenile scats are very attractive, being a lovely red color. However, as with many species, this color fades with age and the adult becomes dowdy in comparison. This species is probably more popular with freshwater aquarists than with their seawater counterparts, but is worth considering for any fish-only tank, as it is hardy and easy to please when it comes to food. Its preference for any foodstuff makes it totally unsuitable for the invertebrate aquarium, however. It is advisable to keep a group of three or so in a large aquarium as they provide a very striking display. Feed this species on any of the usual aquarium fare, including flake and dried food. A lettuce leaf every day would be especially welcome should there by no algae growing naturally in the tank.

SCIAENIDAE

CROAKERS and DRUMS

This is a huge family of 200 or more mainly marine fishes found in all tropical and most temperate seas. The croakers and drums are distinguished primarily by their ability to produce sound. Almost every species possesses an elaborate swimbladder that acts as a sound chamber amplifying noises produced by the adjacent muscles. Sound production is voluntary and seems to increase in the spawning season and after dark. In the aquarium, the fishes tend to become gradually silent as they become familiar with their surroundings. It is thought that this sound-making characteristic has been evolved to aid navigation, borne out in part by the fact that many croakers are found in murky, inshore waters where visibility is poor. Their lateral line often continues onto the tail-fin rays, barbels are present in many species, and the earstones are well developed – all obvious sensory developments.

Considering the size of the family, it may seem surprising that only two have gained any sort of foothold in the aquarium hobby. However, they are not easy to keep and are very fussy feeders needing large amounts of live food to thrive. For the majority of fishkeepers, this demand is impossible to satisfy. They also have characteristically high dorsal fins, which make a tempting target for many other species, causing all kinds of compatibility problems.

Sciaenidae

Although the members of this group have the ability to produce sound, they lose this ability over time.

Equetus acuminatus

Perhaps the hardiest in a family of delicate species.

EQUETUS ACUMINATUS
CUBBYU

   **6**

Sometimes called the High-Hat, this Caribbean species is, perhaps, the hardiest in a family of extremely delicate fishes. It needs a very quiet aquarium; one in which it can conduct its normal, natural business of slowly swimming over the bottom looking for food. It should be kept well-fed on small crustaceans and soft-bodied mollusks. Water quality must be perfect, and this species should never be kept with invertebrates.

EQUETUS LANCEOLATUS
JACK-KNIFE FISH

   **5**

Found in the Western Atlantic, from Bermuda to Brazil, this species lives in deep water down to around 18 m (60 ft) when adult, although the young are found in shallow water. It is extremely fragile in captivity and should never be considered by anyone with less than two years' experience. It needs an inexhaustible supply of live food, perfect water quality and endless patience.

Equetus lanceolatus

Do not even consider this species until you have at least two or three years' experience.

SCORPAENIDAE

LIONFISHES

*T*his large family includes the dragonfishes, lionfishes, scorpionfishes and turkeyfishes. Only the lionfishes are of any significance in the aquarium, however, and only they are dealt with here. As the name scorpionfish implies, these fishes have well-developed venom glands at the base of the dorsal-fin spines, and a puncture wound from one of these spines can be very serious. Although no fatality as a result of a lionfish sting has ever been reported, it has been described as excruciatingly painful. However, after the warning, the reassurance. The venom delivery system of the lionfishes is essentially defensive and is meant to deter larger predators. It is not a means of attack. Indeed, apart from being aggressive predators, lionfishes are very peaceful animals. Despite this peaceful nature, accidents can and sometimes do happen. Great care should be taken when working in the aquarium, as a puncture wound can easily occur if a hand or an arm is accidentally brushed against the lionfish's spines. The venom is a neurotoxin and, as such, is denatured by heat. If an accident does occur, the wound should be immersed in water as hot as the victim can stand. However, this should be regarded as a first-aid measure only, and the victim taken to a hospital emergency ward, along with a note of the scientific name of the species concerned.

In spite of their venomous spines,

lionfishes make excellent fishes for the beginner because they are unusually hardy, easy to keep and extremely long-lived. They are predators, however, and care must be given to their tankmates. Nothing that is smaller than the lionfish should be contemplated, since it can extend its jaws and swallow fishes that seem far too large for it. Moray eels, large groupers, large angelfishes and other lionfishes make the best companions. Although these animals eat live fishes in the wild, they can be

Scorpaenidae
All species in this group have venomous spines and will eat any fish that they can get into their mouths.

weaned onto frozen fishes in the aquarium by mixing dead fish – presented on the end of a length of cotton – with live fishes. The ratio of dead to live can be increased until only dead fishes are being eaten. This process should take no more than two weeks.

Q I have a lionfish which only eats live foods. I find feeding live food distasteful, so what can I do?

A Usually, the importer or the dealer will have trained it before the fish goes on sale. However, you must train the fish yourself. First, you need to carry on with live fish, but start to include some frozen lancefish with them. Suspend the frozen fish on a length of cotton, and jiggle it up and down to make it look like a live one. Gradually, increase the number of frozen fish and decrease the live ones, until the lionfish is eating only frozen fish.

DENDROCHIRUS BRACHYPTERUS

DWARF LIONFISH

Although this lovely little Indo-Pacific species is smaller than most other members of the family, its diminutive size does not make its sting any less unpleasant, so the rules mentioned above apply just as much with this species. It will thrive on a diet of small fishes and other large, meaty foods. A weekly feeding of live river shrimps will be appreciated.

Dendrochirus brachypterus
This may be a small, cute species, but it is still dangerous.

PTEROIS VOLITANS

LIONFISH

Of all the lionfishes this is the most commonly kept in captivity – and the largest. This species is widely distributed throughout the Indo-Pacific, being reported from East Africa to the Western Pacific. It is usually red or brownish, with several dark bands bordered with white. However, it is very variable and even a black form can be found once in a while. As with all lionfishes, this species does well in the aquarium, thriving on small, dead fishes and meaty foods such as mussels. However, it is also a fierce predator that will eat any fish that fits into its mouth. Considering how far it can extend its jaw, this could mean most creatures. It should never be kept with small fishes or invertebrates.

Pterois volitans
The largest and most commonly seen lionfish in the hobby.

Pterois antennata
Common in the Red Sea, this species has white rays on the dorsal and pectoral fins which extend much further than those of *P. volitans*.

PTEROIS ANTENNATA
SPOT-FINNED LIONFISH

 10 | 4-6 | 9

This lionfish is quite common in the Red Sea, although it is also found throughout the Indo-Pacific. The bands on its body are much wider and fewer than those of *P. volitans*, and the white rays on the dorsal and pectoral fins extend much further. The tufts above the eyes also stand out more. It is also much smaller than *P. volitans*. The differences between the species end there, however, as all that has been said in general about lionfishes applies here.

PTEROIS RADIATA
WHITE-FINNED LIONFISH

   10 | 6 | 9

Another species commonly found in the Red Sea, as well as the Indo-Pacific, this graceful creature has elongated white rays on the dorsal and pectoral fins. This lionfish is usually much darker than the rest of the family. Every other aspect described for this family applies equally to this species.

Pterois radiata
Easily identified by the white rays on the fins, this is also much darker than others in its family.

*S*ERRANIDAE

GROUPERS

*T*he sea basses and groupers conjure up a picture of a large, ferocious fish that spends its time looking for other fishes to devour. While that is true with some of the family, there are also small – sometimes delicate – members. The Serranidae is a family of mainly tropical marine fishes, although some are found in temperate seas. Some members of the group live in brackish water. They are mostly fishes of bottom-dwelling habits, although some are active in the surf, and almost all of them live in inshore waters. They are generally large, predatory animals. Some are reported as

Serranidae

Not every member of this family is a large brute – there are some small, delicate species.

weighing as much as 50 kg (110 lb). In general, they are heavy-bodied fishes with wide mouths. Although they have two dorsal fins – the first composed of strong spines – frequently the two are not differentiated by a division in the outline. They have three strong spines in the anal fin and most have fully-scaled bodies, with the lateral line running from head to tail. Many grouper species are hermaphrodites and in some species eggs and sperm develop simultaneously in the same fish, but it is more usual for the juveniles to start life as females, changing to males when the need arises.

This family usually does well in captivity, although some species grow too large too quickly for the average aquarium. Their diet should include shrimps and other meaty foods, with a regular treat of live river shrimps.

Q I really love the Lyretailed Coralfish, *Anthias squamipinnis*, but don't know much about their care. What can you tell me?

A *Anthias squamipinnis* lives in huge shoals in the wild and really is not very strong in captivity when kept singly. Buy a group of five or six and feed them on small foods such as brine shrimps. You will find that there will be one of the group which becomes a dominant male, which is what happens in the wild, as this species is hermaphrodite.

ANTHIAS SQUAMIPINNIS

LYRE-TAILED CORALFISH

This wonderful species – which schools in huge shoals over the reefs of the Indo-Pacific and the Red Sea – has many common names, including Sea Perch, Wreckfish and even Marine Goldfish. It has been largely ignored in the hobby, even being described as difficult to keep. This is mainly because most people buy it as a single specimen, which is doomed to die from the start. This species must have its own kind in the aquarium if it is to thrive. Provided that this need is satisfied, *A. squamipinnis* is as hardy as any other species.

In the wild, each large school adopts a home range near to a coral head, into which it disappears at the first sign of danger. Each school consists of females with one adult male, which can be distinguished by an extended third dorsal spine and different coloration. When this male dies the dominant female will change sex to take its place. Its natural diet is zooplankton (small animals that drift in the current) and this should be reflected in its aquarium diet: brine shrimps and other small, meaty foods.

Anthias squamipinnis

This species swarms over the reef in huge shoals.

Calloplesiops altivelis

A very delicate species which is definitely not for the beginner.

CALLOPLESIOPS ALTIVELIS

MARINE BETTA

This is not a fish for the beginner, since – despite its predatory nature – it is very shy and delicate. It needs excellent water quality and plenty of hiding places into which it can retreat when feeling threatened. When it does, it enters the cave headfirst, leaving its tail and false eyespot waving about. This looks like a moray eel and leaves predators confused and frightened. Care should be taken when choosing tank-mates: no bullies or ebullient species, and no species that is small enough for it to eat. Like the previous species, it should be offered small, meaty foods and loves an occasional feed of small, live river shrimps.

Cephalophelis miniatus
Represents the common image of the grouper and is for large aquariums only.

KEY

LENGTH IN WILD (IN)

LENGTH IN CAPTIVITY (IN)

HERBIVORE

OMNIVORE

PREDATOR

SINGLE SPECIMEN

COMMUNITY FISH

SAFE WITH SMALL FISHES

SAFE WITH INVERTEBRATES

EASE OF KEEPING FOR BEGINNERS (SCALE OF 1–10)   7

CEPHALOPHELIS MINIATUS
CORAL TROUT

*T*his species represents the common image of a grouper. It is a large, predatory species that lurks around, waiting for its next meal to pass by. Sometimes called the Blue-spot Rock-Cod, it is very abundant in some areas of the Indo-Pacific, where it lives exclusively on coral reefs, feeding on smaller fishes that it ambushes from its hiding place. It is not really a serious proposition for the average aquarist because it needs a very large aquarium, and even then it may outgrow it.

Chromileptis altivelis
This species grows to a tremendous size at a very fast rate.

CHROMILEPTIS ALTIVELIS
PANTHER GROUPER

*A*lthough it grows very large very fast, many people regard this species as worthwhile. It makes a fine aquarium subject when young, being peaceful, hardy and easy to feed. Should you decide to keep one, make sure that the filtration system is good as it is a very messy feeder. Feed it as for the previous species.

SIGANIDAE

RABBITFISHES

Closely related to the family Acanthuridae – the surgeonfishes and tangs – this small family of Indian and Pacific Ocean species has been generally overlooked by the hobby. Yet they make fine aquarium subjects – even for the beginner. The rabbitfishes are so called because most, with the exception of the species described below, have a rounded, blunt face reminiscent of rabbits. Although related to the surgeonfishes, they can be distinguished from them by the increased number of venomous spines in the anal fin (seven in the rabbitfishes), two spines on each of the pelvic fins and a forward-facing venomous spine in front of the dorsal fin. They also lack the tail spines of the surgeonfishes. Most rabbitfishes are reef-dwellers that live on algae. In Asia, they are exploited as food fishes although there is a marked reluctance to eat them anywhere else.

In the aquarium they should be provided with plenty of swimming space and there should be a good growth of algae for them to browse on. They do not thrive on substitutes such as lettuce, but will eat most aquarium foods to supplement their natural diet.

Siganidae

Closely related to the surgeons and tangs, this group get the name of rabbitfishes from the round, blunted face which most of them have.

KEY

LENGTH IN
WILD (IN)

LENGTH IN
CAPTIVITY (IN)

HERBIVORE

OMNIVORE

PREDATOR

SINGLE SPECIMEN

COMMUNITY FISH

SAFE WITH
SMALL FISHES

SAFE WITH
INVERTEBRATES

EASE OF KEEPING
FOR BEGINNERS
(SCALE OF 1–10)

Lo vulpinus
The one exception to
the rule in this family,
this species has a sharp
face which earns it the
common name of
Foxface.

LO VULPINUS

FOXFACE

Sometimes called the Badgerfish, this species is the only one of any significance to the aquarium trade. It is a peaceful fish that can be maintained in a community of other, unrelated species, but will fight with its own kind. It cannot be recommended for keeping with invertebrates, as it will usually damage coral polyps and tubeworms. In view of its natural diet, algae must grow naturally in the aquarium if it is to thrive. It will supplement this with the other, more usual aquarium foods.

When introduced into the aquarium, it will very often lose its yellow color for a while. Do not panic. Simply leave the lights off until the next morning, when it should be swimming around normally, looking for food.

SYNGNATHIDAE

PIPEFISHES *and* SEAHORSES

Seahorses are among the most appealing creatures in the sea. However, this is their downfall. How many times have you seen dried seahorses on sale as vacation souvenirs? They also do badly at the hands of the aquarium hobby. Many unwitting beginners cannot resist buying them, even though they have little chance of keeping them alive. In the interests of conservation, the beginner should leave seahorses well alone.

The family of seahorses and pipefishes – which are "straightened-out" seahorses – is distributed worldwide in both tropical and temperate seas. Most species are found in inshore waters and shallow seas, down to depths of 90 m (300 ft), although there are a couple of species that spend their lives at the surface in open ocean. Members of the family have segmented bodies formed by a bony armor beneath the skin. All have tubular snouts and a tiny mouth.

The amount of movement these animals are able to enjoy is necessarily small, due to their rigid armor, and locomotion is effected by means of a gentle wave of the fins. Because of this, seahorses and pipefishes lead very quiet lives. As a general rule, the pipefishes live in crevices in the reef, while seahorses cling onto coral branches or seaweed using their prehensile tails. These animals have strange spawning habits. The female deposits her eggs into a pouch on the stomach of the male, where they are fertilized and incubated. The male then gives birth to the young after two or three weeks.

These animals have a short life. In the aquarium they do best in a very quiet environment – an invertebrate aquarium is best – where there is no competition for food. They need to be fed at least four times a day, on live brine shrimps and live fish fry. As unpleasant as this latter food may be, they need the calcium in the fish's bones. Without it, their bony exoskeleton will go soft.

Syngnathidae
Possibly the most appealing, but also the most abused of all coralfishes.

HIPPOCAMPUS KUDA

YELLOW SEAHORSE

Most seahorses seen in aquarium shops belong to this species, which is widespread throughout the Indo-Pacific. It tends to take on a gray color when first captured, only to turn yellow when it has settled into its permanent home. Do not keep this species unless you are fully experienced and you can provide it with plenty of live feeds every day, a very quiet aquarium with lots of branches to cling onto, and absolutely top-quality water.

Hippocampus kuda

Requires plenty of live feeds on a daily basis.

DORYRHAMPHUS EXCISUS

BLUE-STRIPE PIPEFISH

Like the previous species, this needs optimum conditions to thrive. Having said that, given these conditions, it is a little more hardy than most of its relatives. All of the prerequisites for *Hippocampus kuda* apply to this Indo-Pacific species.

Doryrhamphus excisus

Only optimum conditions will allow this species to thrive.

TETRAODONTIDAE

PUFFERFISHES

Pufferfishes have different names in different parts of the world. In Australia they are called toadfishes or toados, in South Africa, tobies, and in Japan they are fugu. Like the porcupinefishes, they can inflate themselves with water to avoid predators. They differ from that family, however, in that they lack the characteristic spines of the porcupinefishes. The word "tetraodon" means four-toothed and, sure enough, the pufferfishes have a pair of teeth in each jaw, which form a beak. The growth of this beak is kept in check by their natural diet of hard shellfish, a fact that should be kept in mind when compiling their aquarium menu. The flesh of these fishes was once thought to be poisonous, but it is now clear that the gonads, liver, guts and blood are toxic, while the flesh of many species is perfectly safe. However, in Japan, where they eat pufferfishes regularly, there have been cases of poisoning when only the flesh was eaten.

Puffers are found in all tropical and warm, temperate seas, in shallow inshore waters on coral reefs, over seagrass beds and in estuaries. They are not strong swimmers and propel themselves with the dorsal, pectoral and anal fins. In the aquarium they need plenty of swimming space and a first-class filtration system – including a good protein skimmer – to deal with the mess that they make at feeding time. They need to be fed the occasional meal of shellfish, still in their shells, to keep their beaks within comfortable limits.

Tetraodontidae

Depending on where you are in the world, these fishes are called Toadfishes, Tobies or even Fugu.

AROTHRON HISPIDUS

WHITE-SPOTTED PUFFERFISH

Arothron hispidus
Puffers should never be encouraged to inflate themselves, since this imposes a great strain on the animal.

This is probably the largest pufferfish species available in the stores. It has to have a large aquarium with plenty of swimming space. The aquarist should have a first-class filter system in order to keep water quality within reasonable parameters. This Indo-Pacific species, like its relatives, will inflate itself when disturbed.

However, it should never be encouraged to do this as it imposes a great strain on the creature. It should be fed large, meaty items, including the occasional shellfish with the shell left on. If this latter part of the diet is missing, its beak (teeth) will continue to grow until the fish becomes deformed and can't eat.

Arothron meleagris

Pufferfishes are very sloppy eaters and so need highly efficient filters. They go through three color changes during their life cycle.

AROTHRON MELEAGRIS

SPOTTED PUFFERFISH

Like the previous species, *A. meleagris* should never be kept with invertebrates, as it will eat them. Also coming from the Indo-Pacific, it makes a mess when eating, so a very efficient filter system is essential. However, in keeping with most Pufferfishes, it is an extremely hardy animal and can be recommended to beginners without reservation.

CANTHIGASTER SOLANDRI

SHARP-NOSED PUFFERFISH

The fishes in the genus *Canthigaster* are the dwarfs of the pufferfish ranks. However, they have all the characteristics of their larger cousins. This species is also found in the Indo-Pacific and the Red Sea. It is, perhaps, the most striking of the family, being a golden color with a pattern of stripes and spots, and a black spot just below the dorsal fin. It tends to be peaceable when kept with other, totally different species, but should never be kept with others of its own kind. Nor should it be kept with invertebrates.

Canthigaster solandri

Perhaps the most striking of the family.

Canthigaster valentini

A peaceable species, but one which should never be kept with invertebrates.

CANTHIGASTER VALENTINI

VALENTINE PUFFERFISH

*A*nother Indo-Pacific species, this is perhaps the most common *Canthigaster* species seen in captivity. It has the same characteristics as its cousins, and can only half inflate itself when threatened. It has an attractive black pattern over a creamy underside and seems to have a higher forehead than the previous species. This species should be kept like other pufferfishes. A final warning: it will destroy the fins of long-finned species.

Q I have had a pufferfish, *Canthigaster valentini*, for a year. The problem is that its teeth are getting too long for its mouth. What's the answer?

A The answer is to feed your puffer on what it would eat in the wild. That is, hard shellfish, which they feed upon in order to keep their fused, beak-like teeth in check. Try shellfish with their shells still on.

145

TROUBLESHOOTING

Some aquarists consider that the test of a marine aquarist is whether he or she can identify and treat fish disease. A better measure, however, is one who can keep an aquarium full of fish in which disease never occurs. And if your aquarium is properly set up and maintained, disease should not occur. However, disease probably will befall your fishes, especially in the early days, and the more common fish diseases and their treatment are discussed later. First, however, we will look at health rather than disease: how to achieve that health, and how to maintain it in the long term.

Newcomers to the marine aquarium hobby tend to view outbreaks of disease as isolated incidents that affect their fish in an unpredictable way. When outbreaks occur, the usual response is to throw chemicals into the tank in the hope that the symptoms will disappear and, when they do, that the problem has gone for good. The trouble with this reactive approach to disease is that, by the time the symptoms appear, the disease has probably progressed beyond effective treatment.

The pathogens that cause disease in fishes are an ever-present phenomenon on the coral reef, yet bacterial infections or parasitic infestations are hardly ever seen there. This is because, under normal conditions, the animals' immune systems either prevent the pathogens entering altogether, or, if they do enter, they are prevented from reproducing in large enough quantities to cause trouble. Disease breaks out only when the environment deteriorates enough to cause serious stress to its inhabitants.

This stress disables the fishes' immune systems to an extent that allows the multiplication of the pathogens that cause disease. Even though aquarium-kept fishes live in a glass box in conditions that could never claim to replicate those of the coral reef, it is an ecosystem, nonetheless, and the same situation exists. Fishes mainly become diseased as a result of stress. However, whereas most aquarists think of stress in terms of poor conditions, that is only part of the story. Stress can be induced by factors such as aggression, poor diet and lack of compatibility. Fortunately, these issues can and must be addressed if you are to be successful in your

The marine aquarium The successful marine aquarium, once set up and stocked, needs constant maintenance and vigilance to spot early signs of any trouble.

endeavors. The many ways in which stress can be reduced are discussed in Buying and Introducing Fish (page 36).

Fishes are stressed before you even buy them, and may not develop any symptoms until they have been in your care for some considerable time. Given the unavoidable stresses involved in their capture and transportation, every fish should be treated as a biological timebomb waiting to go off in an established community aquarium. And when that happens, it usually has devastating results because infestations can spread very rapidly in the confines of an aquarium.

Diseases in the aquarium are far more easily prevented than cured, and it is considered by many to be beneficial to administer prophylactics as a matter of course. The most popular of these disease-prevention measures appears to be either ultraviolet sterilization or ozone. As we saw in the chapter on filtration, neither will achieve the desired end. Both will only have any effect on free-swimming pathogens, many of which have a lifecycle that includes periods both on and off the host fish. Neither do drugs work as prophylactics. After all, how does the aquarist decide which drug to use or which disease to worry about? The best prophylactic for new acquisitions is to introduce them in the least stressful manner possible.

Possibly the best way to prevent diseases being introduced into the aquarium is to keep fishes under quarantine in a separate tank before introducing them into the main aquarium. This is a common practice among many enthusiasts but, unfortunately, even this is the subject of much debate. One school of thought maintains that the aquarist should keep a quarantine aquarium because the collection in the main aquarium is at risk every time an unquarantined fish is added. On the other hand, others feel that a quarantine aquarium defeats its own object. The aquarist takes great care to buy and introduce a fish into the quarantine tank with the minimum of stress. The fish then spends two weeks or so settling in and becoming used to its new surroundings and to aquarium life in general. When it is happy and feeding, it is then moved again, to the main aquarium and must go through the whole process again.

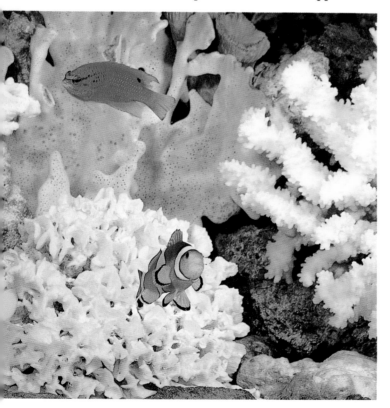

ESTABLISHING AND MAINTAINING A QUARANTINE AQUARIUM

A quarantine aquarium can also act as a hospital tank in which fishes from the established aquarium can be treated, and it should be maintained just like any other tank. However, because coral sand and calcerous rocks have a tendency to absorb substances such as copper – on which many proprietory treatments are based – and release them back into the water at the most inopportune moment, the quarantine tank should be as simple as possible. It does not have to be particularly large. Around 90 liters (20 gal) is adequate, because no more than one specimen should be in it. Filter it using sponge filters driven by an air pump, on which beneficial bacteria can multiply and perform the same task as the biological filter in the main tank.

The aquarium should also contain one or two non-calcerous hiding places. Slate or plastic plants – or a combination of the two – are ideal, but clay pots and PVC tubing will be just as satisfactory. It is also a good idea to keep a small canister filter on hand, filled with activated charcoal, in order to take out

Quarantine tank
This need not be large, but it should, ideally, contain all of the components that make up any other marine aquarium.

any residues of treatment once a course has been completed. Furthermore, many treatments will damage the bacteria in the filter, and the canister filter will come in useful as a backup.

The quarantine aquarium should have its own heater, but it only has to have a small light source. Indeed, it is often beneficial in the treatment of disease for the fish to spend a day or two without any light at all. This will also make shy newcomers feel confident enough to swim around, enabling you to spot any symptoms of disease. It is a good idea to keep a flashlight next to the aquarium, as some diseases, such as marine velvet, are more easily identified when the fish is illuminated from the side. Disease pathogens are highly contagious and separate equipment, including nets, tubing and plastic buckets, should be used for the main tank and for the quarantine tank.

How long a fish should spend in the quarantine aquarium is a matter for debate. Most authorities suggest that two weeks should be long enough for any diseases to manifest themselves, while others reckon on four. The temptation to get your new specimen into the show tank as soon as possible may seem too great to allow you to leave the fish in quarantine for four weeks, but it is better to be safe than sorry.

FRESHWATER BATHS
Freshwater baths have been used by seawater aquarists for a long time because they can be very effective against parasitic infestations. They work so well because they give the pathogens a powerful osmotic shock: the parasites take up water so fast that they explode. However, being dipped into fresh water is also very stressful to the fish. It should be done with great care and only

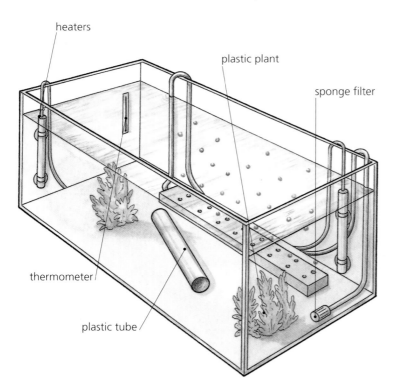

heaters

plastic plant

sponge filter

thermometer

plastic tube

for short periods of time when the aquarist can watch the fish without distraction.

To administer a freshwater bath, fill a 5-liter (14-pint) container — the small goldfish tanks sold by most aquarium stores are ideal — with fresh water from the faucet. This water must be brought up to the same temperature and pH level as the main aquarium before use. It would be best if the water were boiled and then allowed to cool, thereby ridding it of chlorine. To match the pH, add one teaspoonful of sodium bicarbonate. When everything is ready, add 1 liter (2 pints) of seawater from the main aquarium. These preparations will reduce the stress imposed on the animal. To treat the fish, catch it as carefully as possible and place it gently into the bath. The fish will probably lie on its side for a while, but should show no other signs of distress. If it does show signs of distress, it should be put back into seawater immediately. In any event, a freshwater bath should last no longer than 10 minutes, although it may have to be repeated on another day.

GENERAL TROUBLESHOOTING

With one or two notable exceptions, most problems in the aquarium can be traced back to poor water quality, which in turn is usually caused by either a malfunction in the system or lack of care on the part of the aquarist. For example, high levels of ammonia or nitrite are usually the result of overfeeding or overstocking. A high concentration of nitrate shows that too few water changes are being performed, and a low (acidic) pH denotes overfeeding or overstocking.

The beginner must become a good observer. Watch your fishes when they are feeding and whenever you have a moment to relax. Water test kits should be used regularly, but whenever you notice anything unusual, carry out a full check on water quality before anything else. If water quality is found to be lacking, immediate steps must be taken to correct it. If water quality is all right, diagnosis of disease should be the next step.

POISONING FROM OUTSIDE SOURCES

Poisoning causes the fish to behave in a very unusual manner, and they will almost always try to jump out of the water. Cigarette smoke or the use of aerosols around the tank are common causes of external poisoning. If this type of poisoning occurs, the only treatment is to change all the water in the aquarium in 25% batches over three or four days. Heavy filtration over activated carbon is also advisable.

DEALING WITH LOSS OF POWER

First, do not panic, as loss of power rarely last long enough to cause any real problems. However, priority must be given to switching off the equipment. Sudden surges of electricity after power loss can spell trouble for some electrical equipment. The next priority should be to provide air. Small, battery-operated air pumps can be obtained from aquarium or camping stores and it is a good idea to keep two of these — and batteries to run them for about eight hours — on hand in case of emergencies. If you use undergravel filtration, these pumps will at least keep water flowing through it to stop the bacteria from dying. Before power is restored to the tank, any canister filters should be cleaned and refilled because if they are switched off for longer than half an hour or so, they could foul the water when turned on again.

COMMON DISEASES AND THEIR TREATMENT

MARINE VELVET

This often known as Oodinium because the parasite that causes it was known as *Oodinium ocellatum* (now more accurately called *Amyloodinium ocellatum*). This parasitic infestation spreads very quickly, and death follows with corresponding speed. It is also very difficult to treat once it is diagnosed and diagnosis is difficult, as in the early stages the fish carries barely visible gold spots on its body, almost as if the fish has been dusted with pepper. These spots are the juvenile stages of the parasite, which fall off when mature. Each one then divides into as many as 250 dinospores, which can survive for a few days while they look for another host. This, of course, is easy as there is no shortage of fishes in an aquarium. It is this lifecycle that makes it necessary to treat the aquarium as well as the fish.

DIAGNOSIS: An infected fish will breathe very heavily and swim around with its fins clamped to its body. It will also rub itself on rocks continually in a vain attempt to rid itself of the discomfort. This "flashing" can be a symptom of other diseases, so care should be taken in the diagnosis.

TREATMENT: By the time the beginner notices that something is wrong, this disease has usually progressed so far that treatment is extremely difficult. A freshwater bath can help with the trophonts – the spots on the body – and this process is described elsewhere. Meanwhile, the aquarium itself must be treated if a permanent cure is to be achieved. The only truly effective way is to use one of the copper-based proprietary treatments, available from aquarium stores. However, be careful when administering them, since copper is only marginally less toxic to fishes than to the parasites you are trying to kill. Always buy a copper test kit to monitor the amount of free copper in the aquarium, as the treatment may take some time.

LYMPHOCYSTIS

This is caused by the virus of the same name and it can spread to the mouth and prevent its victim from feeding if left unchecked.

DIAGNOSIS: In the initial stages, small, white nodules – looking somewhat like cauliflower florets – appear along the edges of the pectoral fins and the gill covers. As it progresses, it will spread to the mouth and other parts of the body.

TREATMENT: Because Lymphocystis is a virus, there is no known cure. The living conditions of the fish should be improved. The addition of vitamins to the food may also help. Raising the temperature a little to speed up the fish's immune system could also help. However, the only really effective way to deal with Lymphocystis is to cut off the portions of the fins that are infected and bathe the area with an antiseptic solution. There is evidence to suggest that the presence of *Labroides dimidiatus* (Cleaner Wrasse) in the aquarium will greatly reduce the risk of this disease breaking out (see page 86).

FIN ROT

This is caused by the bacteria *Aeronomas*, *Pseudomonas* and *Vibrio*. These are always present in the seawater aquarium, but the immune systems of the fishes will ward them off. Only when the conditions in an aquarium deteriorate badly will these bacteria get a foothold and, as such, fin rot is an infallible indicator of water quality.

DIAGNOSIS: The fins become ragged, and, if not treated quickly, erosion progresses to the base of the fins. In particularly bad cases, even the fish's body around the fin base will start to erode.

TREATMENT: Take immediate steps to restore water quality in the tank. If you have a hospital tank, move the fish to it and treat with Furanace at the rate of 3.8 mg per 4.5 liters (10 gal). Treat for five days, then perform a 50% water change. Meanwhile, raise the water quality in the main aquarium back up to standard. It is useless to use a hospital tank if the water quality in the main aquarium is not good enough. In the absence of Furanace, there are proprietary treatments that will work. Buy those that contain Malachite Green or Acriflavine.

FUNGUS

This can take a hold when the victim is damaged in some way. Again, fungus is an indication of poor environmental conditions, which should be remedied as a matter of urgency.

DIAGNOSIS: Cotton-like tufts around the edges of wounds are a characteristic of fungal infections. Greyish patches could also appear on the site of damage caused by parasites.

TREATMENT: As previously stated, the first job is to improve living conditions in the aquarium. The filter should be cleaned thoroughly and a 50% water change performed. Filtration over activated carbon is also a good idea, and it may even be beneficial to reduce the level of stock in the tank. If you have a hospital tank, move the infected fish into it and treat with a general tonic until the wound is healed and the fungus has disappeared.

GILL FLUKES

Are actually trematodes, usually of the genus *Neobenedenia*. These microscopic worms multiply extremely rapidly.

DIAGNOSIS: A dramatic increase in the gill rate will be accompanied by a loss of appetite. These are symptoms of other illnesses as well, so care is needed over diagnosis. The gills will be pink or gray/white rather than deep red in color. Adult flukes can be seen by the naked eye.

TREATMENT: Gill flukes respond well to freshwater baths and to long baths in Methylene Blue or Praziquantel. Note that fluke eggs are resistant to all therapeutic agents so baths must be repeated within a week to kill off any worms which have hatched in the meantime.

VIBRIOSIS

Another bacterial infection, caused by *Vibrio anguillarum.* It is another indicator of poor conditions.

DIAGNOSIS: Initially, the fish will lose interest in feeding and there will be a loss of colour. These will be quickly followed by fin erosion, and then large open ulcers will appear on the flanks. There will also be a reddening near the vent. At this stage, the animal is close to death.

TREATMENT: This disease will respond to the same treatment as for fin rot, although it is far more virulent and will probably hang around for longer. Early diagnosis is essential if the fish is to be saved, as *Vibriosis* progresses very rapidly.

HEAD AND LATERAL LINE EROSION

This is yet another disease caused by poor environmental conditions, although it is also thought to be a sign of dietary deficiency.

DIAGNOSIS: Species suffering from HLLE, as it is sometimes called, develop holes in the sensory pits around the head and along the lateral line. The fish does not appear disturbed and progression of the disease is very slow. However, osmo-regulation problems may develop if the disease is left unchecked, and the fish will probably die.

TREATMENT: Yet again, immediate steps should be taken to improve water quality. Vitamin supplements and greenstuff in the feed also seem to help.

WHITE SPOT

Also known as Cryptocaryon, is caused by a parasitic protozoan – *Cryptocaryon irritans*. Like marine velvet, white spot has a complicated lifecycle, including stages both on and off the host. For this reason, the treatment is similar.

DIAGNOSIS: While the initial symptoms of white spot are similar to those of Amyloodinium, the spots – which are about the size of a pinhead – are much more easily detected. Should the initial symptoms be ignored, the fish's eyes will become cloudy and lesions will appear on the fins. These lesions can then become a site for secondary bacterial infections.

TREATMENT: Although this parasite has stages both on and off the host, both stages are much more responsive to drugs. However, the fish and the tank need to be treated in the same way for both diseases.

SPECIES TO AVOID

*H*aving discussed the species that can be easily kept by anyone, and those not recommended for beginners, the following are some species that should be avoided by all aquarists owing to specialized dietary requirements, conservation considerations or other reasons. This list is by no means exhaustive, so before you buy any species that you know nothing about, do some homework.

Acoliscus strigatus – Razorfish
Apolemichthys arcuatus – Bandit Angelfish
Centropyge multifasciatus – Multi-barred Angelfish
Chaetodon larvatus – Redheaded Butterflyfish
Chaetodon Meyeri – Meyers Butterflyfish
Chaetodon ornatissimus – Ornate Butterflyfish
Chaetodon trifascialis – Chevron Butterflyfish
Chaetodon trifasciatus – Rainbow Butterflyfish
Dunkerocampus dactyliophorus – Banded Pipefish
Zanclus canescens – Moorish Idol

Selected Glossary of Common Terms

Absorbtion Taking up and holding liquid, as a sponge takes in water.

Activated Carbon Also called charcoal. Used in chemical filtrations to adsorb impurities not removed by other filter processes.

Adsorbtion The process in which dissolved organic material sticks to a substance such as activated carbon and stays there until the carbon is removed.

Algae Primitive plants that can be very simple, single-celled organisms, or massive structures such as kelp. They occur naturally in response to sunlight.

Anal Fin The fin on the underside of a fish, in front of the tail.

Biological Filtration A water purifying system that uses bacteria of the genera Nitrosomonas and Nitrobacter to convert harmful ammonia into nitrite, then into nitrate, and ultimately into free nitrogen.

Brackish Water Water that is neither fresh nor seawater. It is usually 10 percent seawater. Water in estuaries is brackish.

Buffering Potential The ability of seawater to maintain the correct pH, regardless of the loads placed upon it.

Calcareous Formed from calcium carbonate.

Caudal Fin The tail fin.

Caudal Peduncle The part of the fish where the tail fin joins to the body.

Commensalism Two animals live together but one benefits more than the other.

Cover Glass A piece of glass used between the water and the lights to minimize evaporation and to stop fishes jumping out of the tank.

Demersal The spawning action of fishes when eggs are laid on a prepared site.

Denitrification The removal of nitrate using anaerobic bacteria — bacteria that do not require high levels of oxygen — that convert it into nitrous oxide, and then into nitrogen gas.

Dorsal Fin The large fin on the fish's back. There may be more than one.

Foam Fractionation Another name for protein skimming.

Fry Very young fish.

Gills The membranes through which fishes extract dissolved oxygen from the water.

Hydrometer The device used for measuring specific gravity in seawater.

Larvae Newly hatched fishes.

Lateral Line The line of perforated scales along a fish's flanks that lead to pressure-sensitive cells. The fish detects underwater vibrations with this system.

Mimicry The phenomenon whereby a fish resembles another species closely. It is usually done in order to gain a meal or protection.

Nitrification The process of converting ammonia to nitrite and then to nitrate, performed by bacteria.

Osmosis The passage of water through a semi-permeable membrane in order to dilute a strong solution.

Ozone An unstable form of oxygen with three atoms. It is used with a protein skimmer to disinfect aquarium water.

Ozonizer The device that produces ozone using an electrical discharge of high voltage.

Pelagic The spawning action of fishes when eggs are laid in open water.

Phytoplankton Microscopic plants that form part of the plankton. The first link in the food chain.

Quarantine The act of keeping newly acquired fishes apart from the animals in the main aquarium, to protect that aquarium from latent disease in newcomers. The aquarium in which this is done is called the quarantine tank.

Reverse-flow A type of undergravel filtration where the water is first passed through a canister filter before being driven through the filter bed from below.

Subtrate The material used over the base of the aquarium. The sand in the filter bed if you use an undergravel filter.

Symbiosis Two animals live together, to their mutual benefit.

Total system Aquariums with sophisticated built-in filtration and other equipment.

Ventral The underside of a fish.

Zooplankton Microscopic or very small animals that, with phytoplankton (on which they feed), form the planktonic "soup."

INDEX

ACKNOWLEDGMENTS

Key: *a* above, *b* below, *l* left, *r* right

David Allison 22, 36–7, 46*a*, 77*b*, 84*b*, 89*a*, 111*b*, 115, 117, 125, 132*a*, 137*a*, 153; **Arcadia/Jerrard Bros plc** 16*br*; **Ian Took/Biofotos** 78; **Alain Compost/Bruce Coleman Ltd** 96*a*; **Nick Dakin** 59*b*, 91*b*, 122*b*, 123*b*, 126*b*; **Armando Jenik/Image Bank** 80, **Photomax** 2–3, 6, 8–9, 11, 24, 30, 40 42–3, 45, 48, 50–1, 52*b*, 55*a*, 56–7, 58*b*, 59*a*, 60, 62–3, 65*b*, 66*b*, 68*a*, 70, 71b, 72, 73, 74*a* & *b*, 76, 79, 83, 85*b*, 88, 90, 91*a*, 92*a*, 93, 94, 95, 97*a*, 98, 100, 101, 102*b*, 103, 106, 108, 113*a*, 118, 121*a*, 124, 127*a*, 128, 130–1, 133*a*, 134–5, 138, 140, 141*b*, 142, 143, 146–7, 151*l*; **Mike Sandford** 26, 46*b*, 54, 82*a*; **Tahiti Aquariums** 131*l* & *r*; **Tetra** 16*l*, 151*r*; **TFH Publications Inc** 39*b*, 44*a* & *b*, 49*a* & *b*, 52*a*, 53, 55*b*, 58*a*, 61*a* & *b*, 64*a* & *b*, 65*a*, 66*a*, 67, 69*a* & *b*, 71*a*, 75*a* & *b*, 77*a*, 81, 82*b*, 84*a*, 85*a*, 86*a* & *b*, 87*a* & *b*, 89*b*, 92*b*, 96*b*, 97*b*, 99*a* & *b*, 102*a*, 104, 105*a* & *b*, 107, 110, 111*a*, 112*a* & *b*, 113*b*, 114, 116, 120*a* & *b*, 121*b*, 122*a*, 123*a*, 126*a*, 127*b*, 129*a* & *b*, 132*b*, 133*b*, 136*a* & *b*, 137*b*, 139, 141*a*, 144*a* & *b*, 145; **William Tomey** 12, 16*ar*.

All other photographs, diagrams and artworks are the copyright of Quarto Publishing.

Quarto would particularly like to thank Max Gibbs of Photomax at The Goldfish Bowl, Oxford, for help kindly given during the preparation of this book, Dr David Pool at Tetra for supplying products used in photography, and Dr Herbert Axelrod of TFH Publications Inc.

While every effort has been made to acknowledge all copyright holders, we apologise if any omissions have been made.